"NO ONE SPOKE ILL OF HER"
ESSAYS ON JUDITH

SOCIETY OF BIBLICAL LITERATURE

EARLY JUDAISM AND ITS LITERATURE

Number 02

"NO ONE SPOKE ILL OF HER"
ESSAYS ON JUDITH

edited by
James C. VanderKam

"NO ONE SPOKE ILL OF HER"
ESSAYS ON JUDITH

edited by
James C. VanderKam

Scholars Press
Atlanta, Georgia

"NO ONE SPOKE ILL OF HER"
ESSAYS ON JUDITH

edited by
James C. VanderKam

Library of Congress Cataloging-in-Publication Data

"No one spoke ill of her" : essays on Judith / edited by James C.
    VanderKam.
        p. cm. — (Early Judaism and its literature ; no. 02)
        Includes index.
        ISBN 1-55540-671-8. — ISBN 1-55540-672-6 (pbk.)
        1. Bible. O.T. Apocrypha. Judith—Criticism, interpretation,
etc. — Congresses. 2. Women in the Bible—Congresses. 3. Judith
(Jewish heroine)—Art—Congresses. 4. Jewish art and symbolism—
Congresses. 5. Christian art and symbolism—Congresses.
I. VanderKam, James C. II. Series.
BS1735.2.N6 1992
229'.2406—dc20   91-43423
                                                     CIP

Printed in the United States of America
on acid-free paper

TABLE OF CONTENTS

ABBREVIATIONS

AB	Anchor Bible
BA	Biblical Archaeologist
BR	Bible Review
CBC	Cambridge Bible Commentary
CBQ	Catholic Biblical Quarterly
HAR	Hebrew Annual Review
HBC	Harper's Bible Commentary
HTR	Harvard Theological Review
IDB	Interpreter's Dictionary of the Bible
JAAR	Journal of the American Academy of Religion
JB	Jerusalem Bible
JBC	The Jerome Bible Commentary
JQR	Jewish Quarterly Review
LCL	Loeb Classical Library
MGMJ	Monatsschrift für Geschichte und Wissenschaft des Judentums
OTL	Old Testament Library
RSR	Recherches de science religieuse
RSV	Revised Standard Version
SBLDS	Society of Biblical Literature Dissertation Series
SBLSP	Society of Biblical Literature Seminar Papers
TDNT	Theological Dictionary of the New Testament

INTRODUCTION

Some years ago the Steering Committee of the SBL Pseudepigrapha Group decided that, after studying pseudepigraphal books and the Dead Sea Scrolls for the first 15 or so years of its existence, the Group should turn its attention for a while to the Apocryphal or Deutero-canonical books. As a result of that decision, the 1989 session of the Group was devoted to the book of Judith. Six scholars were invited to present papers, and two respondents were appointed to spearhead the discussion. The six participants in order were: Adolfo D. Roitman of the Hebrew University of Jerusalem; Toni Craven of Brite Divinity School, Texas Christian University; Amy-Jill Levine of Swarthmore College; Sidnie Ann White, then of the Albright Institute in Jerusalem and now of Albright College; Nira Stone of the Hebrew University of Jerusalem; and Carey A. Moore of Gettysburg College. The respondents were George W.E. Nickelsburg of the University of Iowa and Richard I. Pervo of Seabury-Western Theological Seminary. A large number of people attended the session, and the discussions that accompanied the papers were lively and thought-provoking.

After the 1989 session the decision was made to gather the papers into a volume so that the larger scholarly world would have access to them. The authors were asked to revise their essays in light of the respondents' comments and the observations made by others who attended the session. The present volume is the result. The reader will note, however, that the list of participants given above and the authors who contributed to the present collection do not coincide exactly. Professor Toni Craven, whose <u>Artistry and Faith in the Book of Judith</u> (SBLDS 70; Chico, CA: Scholars Press, 1983) is mentioned frequently in the essays, was not able to have her paper "Redeeming Lies in the Book of Judith" included because of a prior publishing commitment. However, my colleague Professor William Adler informed me that at the 1988 meeting of the SBL's Hellenistic Judaism Group an excellent paper entitled "Judith as a Hellenistic Jewish Text" was presented by Mark Stephen Caponigro of Columbia University. I then invited Caponigro to submit his essay for inclusion in this volume and he was kind enough to accept the offer.

The book of Judith has proved to be a fascinating object of study and one that can be approached from sundry angles. Its religious and artistic value has, of course, been recognized for centuries. Critical scholars have also been attracted to it. R.H. Charles classed Judith and

1

Tobit under the heading "Quasi-Historical Books Written With a Moral Purpose" in the first volume of his famous two-volume collection <u>The Apocrypha and Pseudepigrapha of the Old Testament</u>. The translator, A.E. Cowley, after summarizing the contents of the work, wrote: "The book is thus almost equally divided between the introduction and the story proper. The former is no doubt somewhat out of proportion, and the author dwells at rather unnecessary length on the military details. In spite, however, of these defects of the composition, the literary excellence of the work is universally recognized even through the uncomely disguise of the Greek translation." (1.242-43) Cowley's comment about the "literary excellence of the work" is most apt and is developed in several papers in this volume. But he, of course, wrote long before the days of the newer kinds of criticism, including feminist readings of texts. Modern scholars, including some whose work is published here, have found Judith to be an especially rich source in this regard. In fact, it is almost too good to be true. It has all of the ingredients of a thrilling story--sex, blood, gore, the triumph of virtue over vice--but besides all these the protagonist is a woman in a heavily male-dominated world. The essays in this volume give some idea of the many sorts of responses the book has elicited from contemporary scholars.

Sidnie Ann White demonstrates that the tale of Judith resembles the story of Jael and Deborah in Judges 4-5 not only in the oft-noted fact that in both a woman saves Israel by killing an enemy general but also in numerous other details of structure, plot, characterization, and form. In her estimation the author had the Jael-Deborah story firmly in mind as he fashioned his novella.

Amy-Jill Levine focuses more on the portrayal of Judith and of her movements in the story. At the beginning Judith, another in a series of feminine representations of Israel, is unusual but domesticated as she leads her pious, widowed existence apart from the other residents of Bethulia. But as she leaves this sequestered existence to move into the public sphere, she becomes a threat to the gender divisions and social hierarchy of her male-ruled world. Consequently, after her victorious return, she must again be removed from that sphere so that her otherness no longer endangers it and so that she can be reintegrated (almost) into the traditional pattern of her society.

Adolfo Roitman studies the character of Achior--the Ammonite general who begins as Israel's enemy, displays an astonishing command of biblical history and deuteronomic theology, and eventually becomes a Jew. He explains that in the story Achior is a double or alter-ego of Judith and documents his case by tracing the descriptions and actions of the two characters through five stages: they begin in opposite locations, assume parallel roles, exchange places with one another, reverse roles, and eventually meet and experience transformations in their characters. Roitman considers all of this a literary expression of the book's ideology of proselytism and isolates some similarities between the experiences of Achior and Abraham, both of whom moved from idolatry or idolatrous contexts to worship of the one God.

Mark Stephen Caponigro revives an older suggestion that the "auctrix" of Judith was acquainted with Herodotus' Histories--a view which he thinks has been unfairly ignored by scholars. He argues that the auctrix borrowed from the narrative structure in Herodotus' account of the Persian invasions of Greece and the battle of Thermopylae and that certain specific details in the text of Judith are better understood if they are seen as less-than-perfect adaptations of points in Herodotus' account. If this is true, interesting questions arise about the auctrix' knowledge of Greek and possibly about the original language of the book.

Carey A. Moore turns to a long-standing question that the fate of the book of Judith poses: Why was Judith, a very "religious" book, not included in the Hebrew Bible, while a "non-religious" work like Esther was? He surveys recent canonical discussions including the demise of the theory that the third division of the Hebrew Scriptures--the Writings--was finally closed at the rabbinic "council" of Jamnia in 90 CE. It is possible that this division was closed already in the second pre-Christian century and that, as a consequence, Judith, which was written in the late second or early first century BCE, was composed too late for inclusion. Nevertheless, other considerations (e.g., historical inaccuracies, the "pro-feminist" stance of the author, the moral deficiencies of Judith's conduct) may also have contributed to its rejection, although there is no definitive answer to the question why the book was not included in the Hebrew canon.

In the final essay, Nira Stone surveys and illustrates the role of Judith and her story in Christian and Jewish art from the ninth through the seventeenth century and beyond. She discusses various examples of how

Christian themes were portrayed through artistic use of scenes from the entire story and through highlighting in various ways--some more detailed than others--the central episode of the decapitation. Later, the triumphant, sword-wielding Judith became a symbol for the more secular themes of courage and patriotic rebellion. However, she also expressed the victory of humility over pride and the triumph of love. In Jewish art Judith became closely associated with the Maccabees and their victory over a foreign oppressor and thus with the images of Hanukkah.

The title which has been given to this collection of essays is taken from Jdt 8:8a (the same wording appears in several English translations of the verse). The sentiment expressed in it seems fitting not only for the book of Judith but also for the present series of papers.

I wish to express thanks to all who participated in the original session, whether by presenting papers, responding to them, or discussing them; and to Mark Stephen Caponigro for his willingness to have his paper included in this collection. In the preparation of the volume, I have received the splendid and expert assistance of Jane Christopherson and Ann Rives of the Department of Philosophy and Religion at North Carolina State University. As always, I am greatly in their debt. Ann Rives was also kind enough to prepare the index. Finally, Professor William Adler is to be thanked for accepting this collection into the series Early Judaism and Its Literature.

James C. VanderKam, North Carolina State University

IN THE STEPS OF JAEL AND DEBORAH: JUDITH AS HEROINE

Sidnie Ann White
Albright College

Judith is one of the most memorable characters in Hebrew literature. In a remarkable story of courage and resourcefulness, she saves her people by one single action that is both compelling and repugnant. Leading female characters are rare enough in Israelite literature to be constantly compared with one another, and Judith has often been likened to Miriam, Deborah, Jael, the wise women of Tekoa and Abel-beth-Maacah, and Esther.[1] And this is not an exhaustive list! I would like to argue that the comparison to Jael and Deborah is neither superficial nor coincidental, but that the author of Judith had the story of Jael and Deborah in the front of his mind as he wrote his story.[2] In fact, in my judgment the author of Judith used the story of Jael and Deborah as the model for the story of Judith.

The first parallel to draw between the stories is the obvious one: a heroine slays an enemy of Israel singlehandedly, by attacking his head. This is, in fact, the correspondence that drew me to the two stories in the first place. However, as I began to investigate the stories, I noticed that many other exact similarities were present, in plot, character and actions. Many of these parallels have been noted by other commentators before me.[3] However, no one, as far as I have been able to verify, has brought them all together in one place. When they are drawn together, I think that it will be plain that the author of Judith used the story of Jael and Deborah in Judges 4 and 5 as a model, and that the actions of the heroine, Judith, parallel the actions of the two heroines in Judges 4 and 5, Jael and Deborah. In this paper I will demonstrate exact similarities in the structure and plot of the stories, the characters of the stories, and certain elements common to both, particularly the song of victory.

At this point I should make it clear that I am assuming that the author of the book of Judith knew Judges 4 and 5 as single unit. Source criticism isolates Judges 5, the Song of Deborah, as a very ancient poetic piece, while placing the prose narrative of Judges 4 at a later date.[4] This is no doubt correct; however, the author of Judith did not use source criticism, and therefore did not separate the chapters. The author read them as one story, and this reading is reflected in the story of Judith.

First, a summary of the story of Judges 4 and 5. The plot is typical of the book of Judges: Yahweh, on account of the people's sin, allows Jabin the king of Canaan to oppress the Israelites. The people cry

5

out for deliverance, so Yahweh stirs up a judge to save them. Now, however, comes an interesting twist: the judge is a woman, Deborah. Deborah sends for her general, Barak, to rouse him for battle against Sisera. Barak and Deborah lead some of the tribes to battle against Sisera, and manage to defeat him. Sisera then flees on foot and comes upon the tent of Jael, identified as the wife of Heber the Kenite, an ally or friend of Jabin. Jael invites Sisera into the tent, covers him with some sort of covering, gives him milk to drink, and, when he has fallen asleep from exhaustion, drives a tent-peg into his skull and shatters it. Afterwards, when Barak arrives, she takes him into the tent and shows him Sisera's dead body. Finally, Deborah and Barak sing a great victory hymn, in which Jael's deed is lauded. This is the story as the author of the book of Judith knew it.

I would like to start my comparison by looking at the structure of the two stories. The story of Jael begins with a political struggle (which has religious implications) between the Israelites and a foreign power, moves to a climax in a private scene between the heroine Jael and Israel's enemy Sisera, which ends in his death, and concludes with a triumphant victory song. The book of Judith uses precisely the same structure. The story begins with a political and religious struggle between the Israelites and a foreign power (chaps. 1-7), moves to a climax in a private scene between the heroine Judith and Israel's enemy Holofernes (chaps. 8-15), and ends in a triumphant victory song (chap. 16). So the overall structure of the two stories is precisely the same.[5]

Now I will move to an investigation of the details of plot and character, beginning with the major characters of Judith and Holofernes, then filling in the details with the other characters. In that way I hope that the detail of the parallels between Judith and Jael and Deborah will be clear.

Judith enters the story at a late point in the plot, as has been noted many times.[6] Craven states that this is not because of lack of skill on the part of the author, but because he has prepared for Judith's entrance by creating an almost unbearable state of suspense through an account of the enemy's seeming invincibility.[7] I would also suggest that the author's artistic decision was influenced by the fact that Jael enters the scene quite late in her story, after the battle and defeat of Sisera's army.[8] Once the heroines appear, the stories move fairly quickly to their climaxes, given the relative length of each. Of course, the story of Judith is much longer and richer in detail than the story of Jael, as befits a free-standing novella.

Once the heroines enter, they are identified. Judith is identified as the widow of Manasseh, while Jael is described as the wife of Heber the Kenite. I will not enter here into the discussion of whether 'ēšet ḥeber means wife of an individual or female member of a certain clan.[9] I would suggest that, whatever the original meaning, the author of Judith would have understood the phrase to mean "wife of Heber." The important thing to notice is that both Judith and Jael are identified as married, but their husbands are, for one reason or another, absent. The same is also true of Deborah, who, in Judg 4:4, is identified as the wife of Lappidoth,[10] an absent spouse. Women, in patriarchal Israelity society, received their identity first from their fathers and then from their husbands, but these women receive their identity from their actions, and, in fact, give identity to their husbands, thus turning the stereotype on its head. In addition, Judith, Jael and Deborah are all, as far as we know, childless, again an unusual state in their societies. Finally, Judith and Jael, by the former's status as a widow, and the latter's membership in a non-Israelite clan, are marginal members of Israelite society. This fact emphasizes the theme in both stories of the weak (symbolized by the female) triumphing over the strong (symbolized by the male) with the help of Yahweh.[11]

After describing Judith, the author tells of her reaction to the bargain struck between Uzziah and the people of Bethulia (7:23-32). She is appalled, and berates the elders for their lack of faith in God. There is no parallel to this speech in the actions of Jael. In fact, one of the major differences between the two stories is that everything is known about Judith's motivation for her action, and nothing is known about Jael's. Here, however, the character of Deborah becomes the model. Deborah and Judith are both firm in their conviction that their actions accord with Yahweh's will. In Judges 4, Deborah makes a speech to Barak, giving him his marching orders and assuring him that Yahweh will be with him. However, she notes in 4:9 that Yahweh will triumph by "the <u>hand</u> of a woman," a motif used throughout both stories.[12] In Judg 4:21, Jael takes the hammer <u>in her hand</u>, and in the victory song in Judges 5 we are told that "she put her hand to the tent peg and her right hand to workmen's mallet" (v 26). In her speech to the elders, Judith says, "The Lord will deliver Israel by my hand" (Jdt 8:33), an unmistakable parallel to Deborah's statement about the hand of a woman. She repeats the statement in her prayer, in chap. 9. Then, at the end of the climactic scene, she tells the people of Bethulia to praise God, who "has destroyed our enemies <u>by my hand</u> this very night" (Jdt 13:14). The motif of a woman's hand creates another similarity between the two stories.

After her speech to the elders, Judith goes to prepare herself for her mission. This too is without parallel in the story of Deborah and Jael (although Zeitlin, among others, has compared this to the story of Esther[13]). Once prepared, Judith summons her maid and they set out for the "Assyrian" camp. Face-to-face with Holofernes, she begins a dialogue that is laced with double-talk and irony. Immediately the parallel with Jael comes to mind. Jael welcomes Sisera into her tent and promises to protect him, all the while intending to kill him. "Turn in, my lord, turn in; fear not" (Judg 4:18). Jael has been taken to task many times for violation of the law of hospitality, while Judith has been condemned for lying.[14] While Jael does violate the law of hospitality, the act should be seen, as Soggin puts it, "in the context of a complex conflict of loyalties."[15] Where does one's loyalty lie? Jael clearly places herself on the side of the Israelites (her name means "Yah is God," thus identifying her with the Yahweh worshipers), and the text celebrates her for that action. As for Judith, her language is deliberately ambiguous. For example, in 11:6, Judith says to Holofernes, "And if you follow the words of your maidservant, God will accomplish something through you, and my lord will not fail to achieve his purposes." "My lord" in Greek is <u>ho kyrios mou</u>. Holofernes assumes she is addressing him, but every Greek-speaking Jew of the period would have heard the Greek translation of "Yahweh" in her words. This use of irony is meant to bring a chuckle of recognition from the reader.[16]

The correspondences now come thick and fast in the climax of the story. In the Assyrian camp Judith is invited to a banquet in the tent of Holofernes. Likewise, Jael invites Sisera into her tent. Holofernes drinks too much wine at the banquet, and passes out drunk. Jael gives Sisera goat's milk to drink, which, as has been widely pointed out, has a soporific effect.[17]

The sexual theme in the book of Judith, recognized by many,[18] is powerful in this scene. Holofernes declares his intention of having sexual intercourse with Judith (12:12). Judith responds to his invitation to the banquet by saying "Who am I, to refuse my lord?", clearly a double entendre! Holofernes, at the sight of Judith, is described as "ravished." Wine is served, and then, at the end of the banquet, the other guests tactfully withdraw, leaving Judith and Holofernes alone. If this were a movie, the screen would be fading to black. However, this is not a movie, and Holofernes soon meets his gory end.

Mieke Bal has argued that the scene between Jael and Sisera is implicitly sexual.[19] Sisera enters Jael's tent. She covers him with a śĕmîkāh (for a discussion of this term, see below). She offers him a special drink, and then covers him again. As he drifts off to sleep (all passion spent?), she murders him. A tie between sex and death is well-known in ancient literature, including the biblical literature.[20] For example, the story of Samson and Delilah presents an instance in which sexual intercourse is closely linked with the death of the man. Even though Judges 4 does not specifically state that sexual intercourse took place between Jael and Sisera, the inference is plausible. I would suggest that the author of Judith makes explicit what is implied in the story of Jael and Sisera. Sensing the sexual innuendos behind the actions of both Jael and Sisera, he chooses to make those innuendos overt in the actions of Judith and Holofernes.

After the men are asleep, the women murder them by attacking their heads, Jael by shattering Sisera's skull, Judith by beheading Holofernes. Boling suggests that the word in Judg 4:21, normally translated as "temple," raqqāh, should be translated as "neck."[21] I am not convinced that there is enough evidence to support the translation "neck"; clearly, though, some vulnerable portion of the skull, not necessarily the temples, is meant. In any case, both Sisera and Holofernes meet their death by means of a head injury. Finally, Judith pulls down Holofernes' bed-canopy (kōnōpion) and takes it with her. The mention of the canopy or curtain here recalls the action of Jael when she covers Sisera with a śĕmîkāh. The śĕmîkāh is a hapax legomenon in Hebrew, and has been variously translated. LXX^A has derrei (skin), while LXX^B has epibolaiō (covering, wrapper). In English it has been translated as a "rug" or a "wooly covering," or it has been identified as the curtain of goatskin which separates the inner portion of the tent from the outer portion.[22] If this latter translation is correct (and there is no conclusive proof one way or the other), then we have a close parallel to the kōnōpion of the Judith story. In any case, we do have a covering motif (a symbol of deceptive security?) in both scenes.

After making her way out of the camp, with the head of Holofernes stored in her food bag, Judith returns to Bethulia, where she triumphantly displays the head to the people of the city. Achior is shown the head of Holofernes and is so astonished and awe-struck that he promptly converts to Judaism. The character of Achior is loosely modeled on the character of Barak in Judges 4 and 5. He is a secondary male character who acts as a foil for the leading female character, Judith, as Barak acts as a foil for Deborah, and later Jael. In the first part of the book of Judith, Achior informs Holofernes that the Jews cannot be defeated because their God protects them, thus enraging Holofernes and setting in motion the central plot of the story. Similarly, Barak's response to Deborah's call sets the action of the story in motion in two ways: when he states that he will not go forth to battle without Deborah, he gives her the opportunity to predict that Sisera will fall by the hand of a woman, thus foreshadowing the action of Jael,[23] and, by leading the Israelites to the confrontation with Sisera, he begins the chain of events that allows Jael's deed to take place. After their initial appearances, both characters leave the stage, only to return after the heroine has completed her action. The parallel is quite clear here. Judith displays the head of Holofernes to Achior, just as Jael displays the body of Sisera to Barak. These events confirm Yahweh's use of a weak, marginalized member of the society in order to save it. Achior is a more fully drawn character, as we would expect in the book of Judith, and he is also a foreigner, which adds an interesting twist to the story. The conversion of Achior, without parallel in Judges 4 and 5, reflects the later date of the book of Judith. In the post-exilic period, membership in the Jewish community was determined by ethnic group and religious affiliation, while in the book of Judges membership in the people of Israel was determined by tribal affiliation. So Achior's conversion is one more symbol of the triumph of Yahweh in the book of Judith, a symbol not possible in the milieu of the book of Judges. Notice that in Daniel 1-6 (which is also post-exilic) the triumph of Daniel is always followed by the conversion of the king. In any case, Achior's function in the story is the same as that of Barak.

Finally, at the end of her story, Judith leads the victorious Israelites in a triumphant hymn to Yahweh. Many commentators have suggested that this hymn is modeled on victory hymns found in the pre-exilic literature, most notably Exodus 15 (the Song of Miriam) and, of course, Judges 5.[24] It seems to me that the parallel is clearest with Judges 5, especially if it is realized that the author of Judith used not only Jael as a model for his leading female character, but also Deborah. The structure of the hymns is similar; as Dancy writes: "One notable feature in common between Judith's and Deborah's songs is the way that in both of them the heroine sometimes speaks in the first person, sometimes is spoken of in the third."[25] Again, I would argue that this feature is not accidental. A close investigation of the structure of the hymn is called for.

Both hymns begin in the first person, with a call to bless Yahweh. The language of the Song of Deborah is notoriously difficult and I do not wish to enter into the translation debate here. Unless otherwise stated, I will be using the translation of the RSV. After the initial call to praise, each song continues with a poetic description of the events recounted in the prose narrative.[26] In v 6 of the song of Judith the person of the verb changes from first to third, to describe the action of Judith. In Judg 5:12 the person changes from the first to the second (referring to Deborah), leading eventually to a description of the actions of Jael in the third person.[27] Finally, each hymn ends with the destruction of the enemies of Israel: "So perish all thine enemies, O LORD!" (Judg 5:31), and "Woe to the nations that rise up against my people!" (Jdt 16:17).

Moving from structure to theme, John Craghan has noted the theme of the disruption of nature which appears in both songs: in the Song of Deborah the mountains quake when Yahweh marches from Seir (vv 4-5), and in Jdt 16:15 the mountains shake and the rocks melt at the presence of Yahweh.[28] Patrick Skehan has also noted that vv 13-17, an anthology of praise, contain material found in Judges 5.[29] For example, in v 13 Judith, having switched back to the first person, sings "I will sing to my God a new song." This is similar to Deborah's "I, to Yahweh even I will sing, I will sing to Yahweh the God of Israel" in Judg 5:3.[30] So the hymns contain structural and thematic similarities. The most important parallel to note, however, is the position of each hymn, coming at the end of the prose narrative, followed by a brief epilogue.

The epilogue in Judges 5 is indeed brief: "And the land had rest for forty years," a typical ending from the book of Judges.[31] The ending of the book of Judith, though longer, has a similar message: "And no one ever again spread terror among the people of Israel in the days of Judith, or for a long time after her death." (16:25) So Judith, like Jael and Deborah, brings peace to the land for a generation (forty years indicating a generation in the book of Judges). In fact, the book of Judith seems to embrace the theology of the book of Judges (which is the theology of the Deuteronomist).[32] In his speech to Holofernes, Achior states: "As long as they [the Israelites] did not sin against their God they prospered, for the God who hates iniquity is with them. But when they departed from the way which he had appointed for them, they were utterly defeated in many battles and were led away captive to a foreign country; the temple of their God was razed to the ground, and their cities were captured by their enemies." (5:17-18) The theology of the book of Judges, of course, is clear from its structure: the people sin, which brings on punishment; the people repent, causing God to raise up a judge to save them; during the lifetime of the judge the people obey Yahweh, and the land is at peace. This "obedience brings reward, disobedience brings punishment" covenant theology is exactly the theology of Achior's speech. A second commonality between the book of Judith and the book of Judges is the impermanence of the role of Judith. She comes forward for a specific task, and, when that task is completed, retires from the stage. This model is drawn from that of the judges, e.g., Othniel, Ehud, and Shamgar, and of course, Deborah. Finally, and this is a very minor point, neither the book of Judges nor the book of Judith is placed in a time of kingship. Judges, of course, is part of the pre-monarchical history of Israel, while in Judith the people seem to be under the authority of a high priest in Jerusalem.[33]

Now I would like to point out some parallels not mentioned in the synopsis of the plot. First is the entire absence of miracle in the prose narratives of both stories.[34] Judith and Jael perform their deeds in completely realistic ways; they seize the chance given to them by the moment. At no point in the narrative, up until the climactic scene, is the audience assured that "everything will be all right." Only the awesome assurance of Deborah and Judith, made clear in their speeches, gives that comfort, and that is a matter of faith, not empirical proof. Second, the deeds of Jael and Judith are not explicitly commissioned by Yahweh.

They act on their own; salvation is achieved by human initiative, although Yahweh is credited with the victory. Especially in the book of Judith the heroine's reliance on the guidance of Yahweh is made clear in her speeches and prayers; yet nowhere is it stated that Yahweh told Judith to do precisely what she did. This is even more so the case with Jael, about whose thoughts and motivations we know nothing. This motif of "salvation by human initiative" is often present in the Hebrew Bible in stories about women: for example, both Ruth and Esther achieve their goals through their own initiative.

      Finally, I would like to mention two correspondences which did not figure directly into the comparison of the character of Judith with those of Jael and Deborah. The first concerns the male characters Nebuchadnezzar and Holofernes. Nebuchadnezzar is a king, who appears at the beginning of the story of Judith (1:1-2:13), leaves the action, and never reappears. Holofernes, the leading male character, is Nebuchadnezzar's general but wields considerable power on his own, and it is his defeat which frees the Israelites from the threat of Nebuchadnezzar. The male characters in the story of Jael have similar roles and functions. In the final form of the story, Jabin, the king of Canaan, is mentioned at the beginning of the story but plays no role in the story itself. The leading male character, Sisera, is described as Jabin's general, but he acts as his own agent, and it is his defeat which frees the Israelites from the oppression of Jabin.[35] The fact that this obvious parallel occurs outside of the main plot is further support for the argument that the author of Judith had the story of Jael in mind when he wrote his story. Second, the battle in both stories is followed by a rout of the respective enemies. These routs occur at different points in the narrative: the rout of the Assyrians takes place after the death of Holofernes, while that of the Canaanites happens before the death of Sisera. It is true, of course, that these scenes are common to battle stories. However, a minor similarity like this one points to an overall scheme of parallels that show the author of Judith adhering very closely to his model.

      To conclude, in this paper I have argued, by citing the corresponding elements of two stories, that the author of the book of Judith used the specific story of Jael and Deborah as the model for his story. The comparison begins with the fact that both stories have heroines who save the Israelites by murdering the commander of the enemy forces, and this murder is accomplished by destroying the head of the victim. But the parallels go beyond this central fact to correspondence in structure, plot and character. The sheer number of both large and small parallels makes the theory of the Jael model highly plausible. Nor would this model have passed unnoticed by the readers of the book of Judith. This modeling technique is a good example of the use of earlier biblical literature in the literature of the second-temple period,[36] and demonstrates the high esteem in which it was held at this time.

[1]For example, see George W.E. Nickelsburg, Jewish Literature Between the Bible and the Mishnah (Philadelphia: Fortress, 1981) 106.

[2]The author of the book of Judith is anonymous, and may have been either male or female. Unfortunately, the English language does not have a graceful way to express a neuter human subject; therefore, when it is unavoidable I will use the masculine pronoun to describe the author. This is in no way to be taken as indicating the (proven) gender of the author.

[3]For example, Carey A. Moore, Judith (AB 40; Garden City, NY: Doubleday, 1985); Morton A. Enslin and Solomon Zeitlin, The Book of Judith (Jewish Apocryphal Literature 8, Leiden: E.J. Brill, 1972); John Craghan, Esther, Judith, Tobit, Jonah, Ruth (Old Testament Message 16; Wilmington, DE: Michael Glazier, 1982), et al.

[4]See, for example, Robert G. Boling, Judges (AB 6A; Garden City, NY: Doubleday, 1975) and J. Albert Soggin, Judges (OTL; Philadelphia: Westminster, 1981).

[5]Toni Craven, in her article "Artistry and Faith in the Book of Judith" (Semeia 8 [1977] 75), makes the following statement about the structure of the book: "The form and content of Part I sketch a religious/political struggle over true sovereignty and true deity; the form and content of Part II detail the resolution of this struggle by the hand of the widow Judith." This is true enough; however, as stated above, I would argue that the structure is actually tripartite, with the concluding victory celebrations separate from the Judith/Holofernes section.

[6]J.C. Dancey, for example, says "Now at last with the introduction of the heroine the narrative gets into full stride...." (The Shorter Books of the Apocrypha [CBC; Cambridge: Unversity Press, 1972] 95).

[7]Toni Craven, Artistry and Faith in the Book of Judith, (SBLDS 70; Chico, CA: Scholars Press, 1983) 58.

[8]This has also been noticed by Alonso-Schökel: "The delayed appearance of Judith may be compared to the later appearance of Jael...." (Luis Alonso-Schökel, "Narrative Structures in the Book of Judith." Protocol Series of the Colloquies of the Center for Hermeneutical Studies in Hellenistic and Modern Culture 11 [1975] 4). Of course, when Jael enters the scene the Israelite army has already won the battle; when Judith appears

the Israelites are on the verge of being utterly defeated.

[9]For a complete discussion and further bibliography, see Mieke Bal, Death and Dissymmetry: The Politics of Coherence in the Book of Judges (Chicago: University of Chicago Press, 1988) 211-212.

[10]The question of whether Lappidoth is meant as a proper masculine name has been raised by some. If it is not the name of Deborah's otherwise unknown husband, what is it? Judah J. Slotki lists four midrashic interpretations: 1. It is a nickname for Barak ("lightning"). 2. It indicates her inflammatory speeches and war-like spirit. 3. It symbolizes the divine inspiration which created sparks and flames. 4. She prepared wicks for the lamps in the sanctuary (Judah J. Slotki, "Judges" in Joshua and Judges [ed. A. Cohen; London: Soncino, 1950] 186). The first two interpretations are the ones most often suggested by commentators today.

[11]Mieke Bal, Murder and Difference: Gender, Genre and Scholarship on Sisera's Death (Bloomington: Indiana University Press, 1988) 20-21; Craghan, Esther, Judith, Tobit, Jonah, Ruth, 89. The notion underlying both stories is that these are unusual roles for women. As P.R. Sanday notes, in most cultures "women give birth and grow children; men kill and make weapons" (Sanday, Female Power and Male Dominance: On the Origins of Sexual Inequality [Cambridge: Cambridge University Press, 1981] 5). The violation of these cultural norms by these women may be perceived as dangerous; this is particularly true in the case of Deborah, who has the charisma of Yahweh (this was suggested to me by Dr. William Poehlmann of St. Olaf College in a private conversation).

[12]Patrick W. Skehan, "The Hand of Judith," CBQ 25 (1963) 94-110. The following comments are heavily dependent on Skehan's article.

[13]Solomon Zeitlin, "Introduction: The Book of Esther and Judith: A Parallel" in Enslin and Zeitlin, The Book of Judith, 1-37.

[14]For example, Wayne Shumaker, in Alonso-Schökel, Colloquies, 50, says: "I have compunctions about her [Judith's] methodology." For the question of Jael's violation of the law of hospitality, see Boling, Judges, Soggin, Judges, et al.

[15]Soggin, Judges, 78.

[16]For more on the use of irony in the book of Judith, see Moore, Judith, 78-85.

[17]As Boling puts it, "she duped him and doped him" (Judges, 98).

[18]For a discussion, see Bal, Murder and Difference, 105.

[19]Bal, Murder and Difference, 105.

[20]Stith Thompson titles this folklore motif "Death from intercourse," motif T182 (Stith Thompson, Motif Index of Folk-Literature: A Classification of Narrative Elements in Folktales, Ballads, Myths, Fables, Mediaeval Romances, Exempla Fabliaux, Jest-Books, and Local Legends [vol 5; Bloomington: Indiana University Press, 1955-58] 362). It has been noticed before that the influence of folklore motifs is prominent in Judith. For

example, Mary P. Coote notes "In its basic pattern and motifs the story of Judith strongly resembles a type of traditional rescue story in which a female figure assumes the role of the hero and saves a male figure (or a social group) from captivity" (in Alonso-Schökel, Colloquies, 21). For a further discussion of the folklore influence, see Moore, Judith, 78.

[21]Boling, Judges, 93, 98.

[22]Soggin, Judges, 62.

[23]It is not germane to our purpose to determine whether or not Barak's refusal to go without Deborah is the result of fear. For a discussion of this question, see Bal, Murder and Difference, 45ff., 115.

[24]Craven, Artistry and Faith, Moore, Judith, et al.

[25]Dancy, The Shorter Books of the Apocrypha, 124.

[26]I would reiterate my earlier statement that the author of Judith knew the story of Jael and Deborah in its final form, as it now appears in the book of Judges; he did not separate it into sources.

[27]The song of Judith shifts back to the first person in v 11.

[28]Craghan, Esther, Judith, Tobit, Jonah, Ruth, 124.

[29]Skehan, "The Hand of Judith," 95.

[30]Translation by F.M. Cross and D.N. Freedman in Studies in Ancient Yahwistic Poetry (Missoula, MT: Scholars Press, 1975) 13.

[31]Cf., for example, 8:28. The book of Judges is given its structure by the Deuteronomistic Historian (Dtr).

[32]That is, the theology of the conditional covenant.

[33]Moore, Judith, 50.

[34]Enslin and Zeitlin, The Book of Judith, 42.

[35]James D. Martin, The Book of Judges (Cambridge: Cambridge University Press, 1975) 54.

[36]For other examples of the use of earlier biblical literature in the literature of the second-temple period, see the category "Expansions of the 'Old Testament'" in The Old Testament Pseudepigrapha (vol. 2; ed. J.H. Charlesworth; Garden City, NY: Doubleday, 1985). Many of the books in this category are in a different literary genre than the book of Judith (e.g., Jubilees); however, they do demonstrate the reuse of the biblical text in the second-temple period. The elements in the book of Judith which are not found in the story of Jael and Deborah, such as the conversion of Achior, are motifs which appear in other post-exilic books such as Esther and Daniel.

SACRIFICE AND SALVATION:
OTHERNESS AND DOMESTICATION IN THE BOOK OF JUDITH[1]
Amy-Jill Levine
Swarthmore College

Exegetical studies of the text of Judith have tried to keep pace with its peripatetic heroine. At first, like Judith on her roof, they were located in the relatively rarified atmosphere of historical investigation. Then, just as Judith summoned the Bethulian leaders, so convincing works have called upon predominant forms of literary analysis. And, like Judith trodding that dangerous path to the foreign camp, recent examinations have made forays into the alien territories of feminism, psychoanalysis, and folklore studies. Regardless of the approach, however, Judith the character is usually identified as a representation of or as a metaphor for the community of faith. Although her name, widowhood, chastity, beauty, and righteousness suggest the traditional representation of Israel, the text's association of these traits with an independent woman and with sexuality subverts the metaphoric connection between character and androcentrically determined community. This paper explores how Judith the Jew/ess (Ioudith) both sustains and threatens corporate determination as well as how that threat is averted through her reinscription into Israelite society.

All women are other, as de Beauvoir declares: woman "is defined and differentiated with reference to man and not he with reference to her...He is the Subject, he is the Absolute - she is the Other."[2] But this generic otherness itself neither problematizes Judith's potential to represent Israel nor threatens Israelite society. The community is traditionally represented by female figures ranging from the virgin (2 Kgs 19:21//Isa 37:22; Lam 1:15; 2:13; Jer 14:17) to the bride (Jer 2:2-3; Hos 2:15b) to the whore (Hosea 1-4; Ezekiel 16) to the widow (Lam 1:1; Isa 54:4-8). Rather, Judith's being a woman who nonetheless speaks and acts in the world of Israelite patriarchy creates the crisis. At the beginning of the book, when she is apart, ascetic, and asocial, Judith is merely a curiosity with metaphoric potential. Present in the public sphere, sexually active, and socially involved, she endangers hierarchical oppositions of gender, race, and class, muddles conventional gender characteristics and dismantles their claims to universiality, and so threatens the status quo.[3] Judith relativizes the normative cultural constructions of the community. Her ultimate return to the private sphere and consequent reinscription into androcentric Israel both alleviate the crisis precipitated by her actions and discourse and reinforce the norms they reveal. Yet because her return is incomplete, the threat of the other remains.

Judith appears at first to be a classic metaphor both for the nation and for all women. Not only does her name mean "the Jewess," but also she "is a widow, for the Jewish nation is living at the time of grave danger and affliction, like a forlorn widow."[4] Judith is the text's only named woman character and thus the only woman recognized by its male-defined world.[5] Further, because her name is a generic, its applicability can easily be extended beyond the individual. The women of Bethulia are all like Judith in that each is a "Jewess." Through her name, Judith is associated with gentile women as well. Judith the daughter of Merari evokes and rehabilitates Judith the daughter of Beeri, the Hittite wife of Esau who "made life bitter for Isaac and Rebecca" (Gen 26:35).[6] But this metaphoric identification of Judith with the Jewish community as well as beyond to gentile women breaks down. Judith the woman can only incompletely represent Israel. The community is historically active; women per se are not. Judith is thus both part of and apart from her people.

Metaphoric connections between the heroine and the community extend beyond Judith's name to gender-determined categories. Yet gender alone does not define their common characteristic. Israel's traditional representations as virgin, continent bride, adulterous whore, and celibate widow also share a sexual thematic. Faithful Israel is sexually controlled; her faithless antitype is sexually loose. Consequently, the chaste widow Judith - like the virgin Dinah (Jdt 9:9-10) - represents the holy community. Yet the connection between widow and virgin is severed as Judith's rhetoric unties the lines identifying her with both Israel and other women. The initial prayer in chap. 9 identifies the rape-victim Dinah by a generic term; she is called simply a "virgin" (...parthenou, 9:2). But unlike "Judith", this generic does not function as a proper name. Dinah has been robbed of her personhood. Further, Judith equates Dinah's rape with the siege of Bethulia, and the association is reinforced by the resonance between the name of the town and the Hebrew for "virgin," btwlh.[7] Judith, however, assumes the man's role of protector-avenger associated with her ancestor (cf. 9:2,...tou patros mou symeon). Indeed, like Simeon she expresses no sympathy for the Shechemite

women.[8] That the deity "gave their wives for a prey and their ç
captivity" (9:4) Judith interprets as a sign of divine justice. Mention
these victims occurs in the context of social egalitarianism - the deity
"strikes slaves as well as princes" (9:3) and is called the "god of the lowly,
helper of the oppressed, upholder of the weak, protector of the forlorn,
savior of those without hope" (9:11) - but Judith herself does not recognize
gentiles as in need of protection. Were Judith fully to embody Israel, then
the traditional representation of the deity as the (male) savior of the
female-figured community would be challenged. Were all women to be
like Judith, not only Holofernes would lose his head. Were Judith to
represent gentile women, then the paradigmatic identification of Israel as
chosen from among the nations would be compromised. Such separation
of Judith from corporate Israel, from Jewish women, and from gentiles
preserves the text's patriarchal ethos.

re read

While Judith's widowhood conforms to the traditional
representation of Israel as a woman in mourning and while both she and
Bethulia are draped in sackcloth, Judith's particular representation - her
status, rhetoric, wealth, beauty, and even her genealogy - aborts the
metaphor.[9] This widow is hardly the forlorn female in need of male
protection. Given the negative associations of her husband's name,
Manasseh, his absence is almost welcome; he shares the name of the king
held responsible for the Babylonian exile (2 Kgs 21:12-15; 23:26-27; 24:3-
4). Moreover, the circumstances of his death, heatstroke while watching
the binding of barley sheaves, graphically anticipate the decapitation of
Holofernes. The phallic imagery of the bound sheaves prefigures the
general's dismembered head; both symbolize castration.[10] The
psychosexual suggestiveness of this imagery is complemented by barley
meal's ritual function; it is the offering required of a man who suspects his
wife of infidelity even "though she has not defiled herself" (Num 5:15).
Linguistic parallels make the ties between Manasseh and Holofernes even
more pronounced. While the general is decapitated by Judith, Manasseh
is cut down when the burning fever attacks his head (kai ho kausōn ēlthen
epi tēn kephalēn autou). Each man takes to his bed (kai epesen epi tēn
klinēn autou [8:3] kai Olophernēs propeptōkōs epi tēn klinēn autou
[13:2]), and each dies. Manasseh's absence is necessitated by the demands
of Israelite patriarchy: Judith's actions would have subjected him, had he
been alive, to sexual disgrace.[11] Only Holofernes realizes the danger of

humiliation: "It will be a disgrace if we let such a woman go without enjoying her company, for if we do not embrace her she will laugh at us" (Jdt 12:12). By her sexually charged presence, the widow Judith therefore threatens the masculine ethos of the Assyrian army.

The specified length of Judith's mourning has been claimed "to heighten the picture of her loyalty and devotion" to her dead husband,[12] but the reference to "three years and four months" or forty months (8:4) is overdetermined. The length of her mourning and the meaning of her widowhood extend beyond concern for the absent spouse. First, the period recapitulates the forty years Israel spent in the wilderness. From the time of the Passover/the barley harvest, Judith undergoes a period of testing and purification. But this analogy does not require her to mourn for Manasseh any more than the generation in the wilderness needed to mourn for Egypt. Second, the three years and four months structurally parallel the thirty-four days of the siege (7:20). Third, the detailed description of Judith's mourning stresses her otherness. Upon her husband's death, Judith removed herself from Bethulian society and specifically, from men.

Judith had to be a widow - that is, sexually experienced but unattached - in order for her to carry out her plan. And she had to stay a widow. Upon completing the festivities in Jerusalem, she "went to Bethulia, and remained on her estate... Many desired to marry her, but she remained a widow" (16:21-22). Remarriage for levirate purposes would create a new lineage and consequently challenge the power structure of Bethulian society. Further, as a widow safely returned to her proper place, the private sphere, Judith preserves her identification with Israel: no longer active, she no longer subverts the metaphor. A utilitarian reading would even claim that Judith remains a widow both because she had nothing to gain by marriage and because no man was worthy of her. Only the text's females act in a fully efficacious manner;[13] only Judith displays well-directed initiative; only her maid competently follows instructions. The men are weak, stupid, or impaired: Manasseh dies ignominiously: Holofernes is inept; Bagoas is a eunuch; Achior faints at the sight of Holofernes's head. Uzziah, who shares Judith's ethnicity and elevated social status and who, because he is descended from Simeon, might even be able to claim levirate privileges, is the biggest disappointment. Judith must correct his naive theology, and she stands

firm while he wavers in his faith (cf. 7:30-31).[14] The only fit male
companion for Judith is the deity, and it is with him she communes in
prayer on her roof. Yet given the lack of his direct presence in the text,
this relationship is a bit one-sided. Indeed, Coote has argued that Judith
"represents a kind of reversal of the type of rescue pattern underlying the
exodus story, in which a male hero (the Lord) rescues a female figure
(Israel) from captivity."[15] Rather than conform to the traditional image of
widow, Judith's representation follows both divine and male paradigms.

Like her name, gender, and widowhood, Judith's genealogy
betrays her metaphoric function. This list is not an invention designed to
mock the elaborate pedigrees fabricated by post-exilic aristocrats (so
Bruns), nor is its purpose primarily to indicate Judith's Samaritan origins
(so Steinmann).[16] On the one hand, the genealogy anchors Judith to
Israelite history. The reference in 8:1 to "Israel" reinforces the symbolic
value of Judith's own name. Further, as the connection to Israel (=Jacob)
signals Judith's talents for deception and for crossing boundaries, so
names like Gideon, Elijah, Nathaneal, Joseph, and Merari portend her
abilities to function in such roles as judge, prophet, ambassador, and
priest. She supersedes her genealogy and so her generation's
representative of "Israel." On the other hand, because neither the Israel
of 8:1 nor any of the others listed in her family tree has made his mark in
history - they, unlike Judith, have not lived up to their names - the
inscription of each in history is due entirely to her. She is the one who also
reinscribes the branch of her family that had been written out (Jdt 9:2; cf.
Gen 49:7 as well as the silence in Jdt 8:1-2): the line of Simeon. Thus,
while Judith's genealogy situates her within the historical community and
makes her its representative, it is Judith herself who confers value,
meaning, and legitimacy to those whom she represents. The relationship
between the representation (i.e., Judith) and the represented (i.e., her
historical community) which undergirds any metaphoric identification is,
consequently, rendered problematic.

In terms of her relationship to the present generation of
Bethulians, Judith is marked as other by her wealth, beauty, and
religiosity. Rich, gorgeous, pious, as well as independent, Judith is
particularly distinguished from others of her sex. The women in Bethulia
are weak from thirst, robbed of their voice by their husbands (cf. 4:12),
and controlled by the town leaders (7:32b). Even Judith's maid lacks her

freedom. These distinctions are first established through a geographical notice with attendant value hierarchies. Judith is defined spatially as superior to the rest of Bethulia: the "women and young men" are associated first with the "streets of the city and...the passages through the gate" (7:22); she is on her roof (8:5). They are unsheltered and in need of protection; she is in a tent and is, additionally, either unaware of or unconcerned with the danger below: she distributes neither her wealth nor her water. Instead, her wealth allows her to enhance her beauty and so further distinguish herself: she has water for bathing while the people are fainting from thirst (7:22). The text then dwells on the material goods available for her adornment: "She bathed her body with water and anointed herself with precious ointment...and put on a tiara, and arrayed herself in her gayest apparel...and put on her anklets and bracelets and rings and her earrings and all her ornaments..." (10:3b-4). Originally she was "beautiful in appearance, and had a very lovely face" (8:7); now she rivals Helen of Troy. Chabris and Charmis notice "how her face was altered" (10:7), and to the men in the Assyrian camp she was "marvelously beautiful" (10:14). Even Judith herself acknowledges the striking "beauty of her countenance" (16:7). The enemy soldiers "marveled at her beauty, and admired the Israelites, judging them by her..." (10:19). Although they mistakenly perceive Judith as representing her contemporaries - only Judith possesses such striking beauty - the soldier's judgment supports Judith's identification as a traditional metaphor of Israel.

Judith's piety also supports her metaphoric identification with Israel even as it severs her connection to the Bethulian population (8:5-6, 28-29, 31; 9:1-14; 10:2, 8; etc.). No fanatical ascetic, the truly observant widow demonstrates her faith both by fasting and by eating at appropriate occasions (a trait that will serve her well in Holofernes's camp). This religiosity is distinguished from the bad theology and related practices of the Bethulian leaders. The men return to their posts (8:36), but Judith engages in devotional activities "at the very time when that evening's incense was being offered in the house of God in Jerusalem" (9:1). As a woman, she is technically marginal to the operation of the official cult. But on her roof, she can participate in devotions without endangering the status quo. Close to the deity in spirit and in physical location, she is removed from the people both religiously and spatially. The summary verse of her introduction (8:7-8) confirms her various unique attributes and retains the emphasis on her piety. While her beauty plus the "gold and silver, and men and women slaves, and cattle, and fields" left to her by her husband would be sufficient to distinguish her from other Bethulains, "no one spoke ill of her because (hoti) she feared God exceedingly" (8:8).

When the woman of whom the community spoke chooses herself to speak to them, she unleashes otherness into the public sphere. By sending her female slave out of the female-defined household into the male-dominated public sphere, Judith weakens the gender divisions defining Israelite society; by conveying Judith's summons to the town leaders, the female slave inverts social hierarchies. These inversions continue throughout Judith's contact with men in positions of power. By accepting Judith's theological program, the Bethulian leaders both reinforce her metaphoric potential to represent the faithful community and acknowledge her potentially subversive voice. When they endeavor to redirect her discourse toward piety (8:31), she makes public her intent to act; they are reduced to accepting her words (8:33-34; 10:9). And those words subvert the metaphoric understanding of language in the public sphere - the sharing of a common code - just as her actions subvert her metaphoric identification with Israel. For example, Judith promises "to do a thing which will go down through all generations of our descendants" (8:32), but her "thing" (pragma) is a sign lacking any definitive referent. In the Assyrian camp, Judith continues to transgress linguistic expectations. Her use of double entendres (e.g., the double referents to "lord" [kyrios] in 11:5, 6, 11; 12:14) furthers her subversive intent.

Exploitation of conventional expectations is indicated by more than Judith's rhetoric. According to Alan Dundes, when Judith removes "the garments of widowhood and mourning (10:3) to wear attractive alluring garb [she] appears to move metaphorically from death to life."[17] Yet this is one more metaphor Judith undercuts, for the "life" into which she moves is of a very peculiar sort. The private widow becomes a public woman; she undergoes a total inversion from ascetic chastity to (the guise of) lavish promiscuity. Nor does she simply enter the life of the community either through association with her neighbors or through levirate marriage; rather, she leaves town. Finally, she moves not directly from death to life but rather from death of one sort, that of the widow separated from her besieged and dying society, to death of another, that of the assassin active among a doomed population. The Assyrian camp is the realm of the dead: characterized by killing and populated by the castrated Bagoas, the beguiled, the besotted, and the beheaded. That Holofernes's "god" is the "historically dead" Nebuchadnezzar and that the army represents the "historically conquered" Assyrian empire further denies the gentiles any association with life. Only when Judith returns to her people and celebrates with them in Jerusalem does she both create and enter the realm of life. But at that moment, tainted by death as well as confirmed as a dangerous other active in the public sphere, she threatens the structure of the very life she engenders and upholds.

Upon her return, the seeds of Judith's threat begin to flower in Israel. By her actions and by her presence, she offers those previously marginal to or excluded from the power base - Jewish women, Achior the gentile, the maidservant - roles in society and cult. The conditions under which gender-determined, ethnic, and class-based integration occur, however, differ according to the text's treatment of women, proselytes, and slaves. Before Judith entered the Israelite public sphere, the Jewish women were separated from their husbands and from the place of action by their leaders' command (7:32). In 15:12-13, "all the women of Israel" (pasa gynē Israēl) gather to see her and bless her; some even dance in her honor. In turn, she distributes branches (thyrsa) to her companions.[18] These women, who then "crowned themselves with olive wreaths," reveal their transformation into active agents. Last, Judith leads "all the women" (pasōn tōn gynaikōn) while "every man" (pas anēr Israēl) followed them. Thus the female population of Israel, like the sword-brandishing (13:6-8) and head-bearing (13:15) Judith, become both graphically and by their actions phallic women.[19] Such inversions of male-female leadership patterns are permitted if not necessitated by the extraordinary circumstances of Judith's deed and Israel's rescue. However, they cannot be allowed to continue unchecked. Only by remaining unique and apart can Judith be tolerated, domesticated, and even treasured by Israelite society. The women consequently must return to their home and their husbands.

Just as Judith transforms the social roles of the Israelite women, so she transforms the life of the gentile Achior. Like Rahab before him and like Judith herself, Achior's name and reputation remain alive among the people (14:10). However, because Achior is male, this new social and religious position can be marked on his flesh as well as in his new community. The gentile man's incorporation into Israel is the inverse of the Jewish woman's position in the Assyrian camp.[20] Achior becomes a Jew first by sharing a meal with the leaders of Bethulia and second, primarily, through his circumcision. Judith too is physically altered (10:7) in preparation for incorporation into the alien community, but her mark of difference is not permanent: the makeup is washed off each night. Similarly, Judith refrains from becoming "like the daughters of the Assyrians" (12:13) by refusing Holofernes's food. Finally, Achior's incorporation into the Jewish community is confirmed by his singular movement. Unlike Judith, who moves back and forth from populated areas to liminal sites, Achior moves only to Israel. While Judith thus is figured as other to both Jew and gentile, Achior the convert mediates between the two.

Although gender-determined and ethnic integration occur during the course of the narrative, incorporation of Judith's servant does not. On the one hand, she appears to be Judith's double: linguistically, habra is related to habras - "graceful, beautiful" - which could serve as Judith's other name. Similarly, Judith adopts for herself in 11:5-6 titles of subservience - slave (doulē) and handmaiden (paidiskē [which can connote "prostitute"]) - used elsewhere for her maid (paidiskē in 10:10, doulē in 12:15; 13:3). Yet, on the other, the patriarchal culture can deal with only one woman who speaks and acts; another such exceptional individual would too severely compromise the status quo. Thus, until Judith's death, her "favorite slave" must remain silent and in service.

The relationship between Judith and her maid is ironically paralleled by that of Holofernes and his eunuch. In Jdt 12:11, Bagoas is described as in charge of Holofernes's personal affairs; we have already been told that the maid oversees Judith's estate. Further, Bagoas summons Judith just as the maid summoned the leaders of Bethulia. In 13:3, both maid and eunuch receive the same instructions. But the parallelism is dramatically incomplete. Bagoas is the only named character in the text who is not somehow brought into Judith's community. Incorporation is accomplished if the act of severing or sacrifice - of the past, of the gentile community, of one's foreskin - is brought about by the Jews themselves and serves the needs of their community. The form of incorporation in turn supports the text's concern with gender roles. Circumcision and that for which it substitutes, castration, both call attention to sexual difference rather than to undifferentiated integration. This difference is necessary for social organization and so for preservation of the status quo, as the removal of Judith from the public sphere and the return of the Bethulian population to their normative lives indicate. Achior, who as circumcised accepts sexual difference, fits into the community. So does Holofernes, once he is dead, since his (symbolic) castration would otherwise deny that difference. The eunuch, who as castrated but alive problematizes sexual difference, does not fit into the community.

Because she muddles sexual difference through her inversion of gender roles, Judith cannot as easily as Bagoas be erased from the story. She must somehow be domesticated, and this is done in part through representations of the other which evoke Judith yet which lack her subversive force. Achior's conversion, the presence of Holofernes's head, the maid's freedom and, especially, the stories people tell about the pious widow all substitute for Judith.[21] They serve to maintain her presence in the public sphere while concurrently displacing her threat. The future is thereby protected. To preserve the status quo and to restore the sexual difference that determines it, Judith's actions must also be rendered kosher. Her concluding psalm reinforces traditional gender roles first by stressing the irregularity of conquest by the "hand of a female" (thēleia)[22] and second by giving full glory to the deity. Next, Judith submits to priestly ministrations (16:18); at this time, she also gives up the evidence of her time in the Assyrian camp: "Judith also dedicated to God all the vessels of Holofernes, which the people had given her; and the canopy which she took for herself from his bedchamber she gave as a votive offering to the Lord" (16:19). This celebration in Jerusalem (16:18-20) reappropriates the sacrifice in 13:6-9. The initial ritualized killing, which included the purification and festive garbing of the celebrant, her sexual abstinence, the painless slitting of the victim's throat (he being "overcome with wine" [13:2]), the aid of the assistant in disposing of the parts, the retention of a portion of the sacrifice for the community, and the efficacy that such an offering brings to Israel as a whole is given its full value only when the account - and the vessels, the canopy, and the general's head - become part of the communal celebration. Moreover, the sacrifice in Judith 16 makes proper the parodic event in 13: Judith's victim is an inappropriate offering; she is not a priest, and the killing required two strokes. The heroine's direct links to the divine, coupled with her temple-oriented piety, suggest she plays the man's role of priest as well as of warrior. But, because such subversion of gender roles threatens Israelite society, her sacrificial and military actions must be constrained and contained.[23] Through the rewriting of her sacrifice as well as the sacrifice of the tokens of her deed, her transgressions are expiated.

Then, Judith herself must leave the public sphere, and life must return to normalcy. No longer the united "people" (cf. ho laos in 16:20) comprised of men and women, now "each man (hekatos) returned home to his own inheritance, and Judith went to Bethulia and remained on her estate" (16:21). The women, so prominent during the celebration, are completely erased. The inversion of gender roles is ended, and the status quo is reinforced. But even in her return, Judith resists complete domestication. Because she is not described as reentering the lifestyle described in 8:4-6[24] - she returns to her estate (16:21), but no mention is made of her earlier ascetic religiosity - she becomes other to her past. Her activities in the public sphere have thus not only changed the fate of the Bethulian population, they have changed Judith herself. On her estate but not on her roof, and in touch with the local population (as one might conclude from the mention of the repeated proposals), Judith is not comparably closer to the Bethulian society she already once disrupted. Like Holofernes, the only way Judith will no longer directly threaten ordered (i.e., gender-determined) Israelite society is through sacrifice, severing, and death.

Judith's distribution of property, her death, and her burial may be seen as inverse images of Achior's circumcision and Holofernes's decapitation. Complete incorporation requires a sacrifice with attendant communal benefits, and Judith in death conforms to this textual rubric. Because she is not male, she can neither lose her foreskin nor, given the metaphoric connection between decapitation and circumcision, her head. Judith has only two possessions which could be sacrificed: her property and her life. Given the threat even her reputation poses to the community, it is not inappropriate that she surrender everything. Consequently, "she set her maid free. Before she died she distributed her property" (16:23, 24). Then, Judith's only remaining public appearance is her burial; not surprisingly, 16:23 explicitly notes that "they buried her in the cave of her husband, Manasseh." In death, she is made to conform to her traditional role as wife.

All that remains of the intrusion of Judith's otherness into the public realm is her "fame" (16:23). That is, her deed becomes incorporated into public memory and public discourse, and it is thereby controlled. Yet each time her story is told, this woman who represented the community as well as exceeded that representation, will both reinforce and challenge Bethulia's - and the reader's - gender-determined ideology.

---

[1]A revised version of "Character Construction and Community Formation in the Book of Judith," SBLSP (ed. David J. Lull; Atlanta: Scholars Press, 1989) 561-69. I am grateful to Laura Lomas, Laura Augustine, Emily Stevens and especially, Jay Geller, for their numerous insightful criticisms and suggestions on earlier drafts, and to George Nickelsburg, Richard Pervo, and David Halperin for their helpful comments on the seminar paper.

[2]Simone de Beauvoir, The Second Sex (New York: Bantam, 1961) xvi.

[3]Jonathan Z. Smith, "What A Difference A Difference Makes," "To See Ourselves as Others See Us": Christians, Jews and "Others" in Late Antiquity (ed. J. Neusner and E.S. Frerichs; Chico, CA: Scholars Press, 1985) 36: "The 'other' emerges only as a theoretical issue when it is perceived as challenging a complex and intact world view." At this point, the different becomes both alien and dangerous. Cf. James G. Williams, Women Recounted, Narrative Thinking and the God of Israel (Sheffield: Almond, 1982) 78: Judith "captivates Holofernes and the Assyrians in a fashion reminiscent of the wisdom tradition's warnings against...the 'alien woman' (Prov 6.24-25; Sir 9.8-9; 25.21)." While Smith notes that "Difference most frequently entails a hierarchy of prestige and a concomitant political ranking of superordinate and subordinate" (4-5), he does not classify women among his proximate others. Feminist criticism, which posits gender as a prime matter of inquiry, suggests that by her very difference, woman challenges traditional methodological and epistemological perspectives. See, among others, Elaine Showalter, "The Feminist Critical Revolution," The New Feminist Criticism (ed. E. Showalter; New York: Pantheon, 1985) 3-10; Gayle Greene and Coppelia Kahn, "Feminist scholarship and the social construction of woman," Making a Difference, Feminist Literary Criticism (ed. G. Greene and Coppelia Kahn; London and New York: Methuen, 1985) 1-36.

[4]L. Alonso-Schökel, "Judith," HBC 810; cf. his "Narrative Structures in the Book of Judith," Protocol Series of the Colloquies of the Center for Hermeneutical Studies in Hellenistic and Modern Culture 11 (ed. W. Wuellner; 1975) 14-15: "As a widow, [Judith] can represent the Jewish people in her affliction"; "as a weak woman lacking the support of her husband, she can show and reveal better the force of God (9:10-11; 13:14-15; 16:6)." Cf. even Luther's comment that "Judith is the Jewish people, represented as a chaste and holy widow" (cited by, inter alia, T. Craven, "Artistry and Faith in the Book of Judith," Semeia 8 [1977] 77). On the connection of Israel/the Jewish nation and Judith see also Craven, Artistry and Faith in the Book of Judith (Chico, CA: Scholars Press, 1983) 85; D.R. Dumm, "Judith," JBC 626. On the name's allegorical potential see Williams, Women, 76, representing literary-critical reading; M.P. Coote, "Comment on

'Narrative Structures in the Book of Judith'," Colloquies, 21-22, on the significance of the name for the female warrior; and C. Moore, Judith (AB 40; Garden City, NY: Doubleday, 1985) 179.

[5]Jdt 8:1 breaks the pattern of the first seven chapters, in which a plethora of male names and so individual male subjects appear. Alonso-Schökel sees the break caused by the genealogy in terms of plot rather than gender: it interrupts the campaigns of Holofernes and Nebuchadnezzar ("Narrative Structures," 4).

[6]Noted by E. Bjorkan, "Subversion in Judith: A Literary-Critical Analysis" (Senior Thesis, Swarthmore College, 1987) 53. One should add to Bjorkan's work the further connection between the two women: neither has children.

[7]Inter alia, Alonso-Schokel, "Judith," 806, and his less sanguine comments in "Narrative Structures," 18-19.

[8]Cf. the possible contrast to Dinah, who "went out to visit the women of the land" (Gen 34:1).

[9]Ironically, the Mishnah's description of widows fits Judith better than the literary metaphor. On the autonomous widow, see the excellent discussion by Judith Romney Wegner in Chattel or Person? The Status of Women in the Mishnah (New York and Oxford: Oxford University Press, 1988) esp. 138-43.

[10]On the relationship between decapitation and castration see Alan Dundes, "Comment on 'Narrative Structures in the book of Judith,'" Colloquies, 28-29. The tie between decapitation and genital mutilation adds another dimension to the well-known trope connecting Holofernes with Shechem, and Judith with Dinah/Simeon.

[11]See W. Shumaker, "Critique of Luis Alonso-Schokel on Judith," Colloquies, 32.

[12]M.S. Enslin, The Book of Judith (Jewish Apocryphal Literature 8; Leiden: Brill, 1972) 111.

[13]Commenting on 15:11, Craven (Artistry, 104 n. 73) observes: "The text reads ten hemionon, "mule" in the singular... Could it be that Judith's female donkey, like Judith herself, can do what it usually takes a team to do?"

[14]Cf. Toni Craven, "Redeeming Lies in the Book of Judith," paper presented to the Pseudepigrapha Section, AAR/SBL Annual Meeting, Anaheim, 1989.

[15]"Comment," Colloquies 21. Such a reversal endangers both the tradition and the status quo.

[16]J.E. Bruns, "The Genealogy of Judith," CBQ 18 (1956) 19; M. Steinmann, Lecture de Judith (Paris: J. Gabalda: 1953) 72.

[17]"Comment on 'Narrative Structures,'" Colloquies 28.

[18]The combination of the thyrsa with the decapitated head and the women's celebration is strongly reminiscent of the Bacchae, another story in which gender-roles are muddled

and in which an "other" is both dangerous and desirable.

[19]J. LaPlanche and J.-B. Pontalis, The Language of Psychoanalysis (New York: Norton, 1973), define the phallic woman as one "endowed, in phantasy, with a phallus." In one such phantasy, she is "represented...as having an external phallus or phallic attribute" (311). The identification is often applied to threatening women manifesting "allegedly masculine character-traits" (312).

[20]For a discussion of the parallels between Judith and Achior, see Adolfo D. Roitman's essay, "Achior in the Book of Judith: His Role and Significance," in this volume.

[21]Cf. Coote, "Comment," Colloquies 26: "It is often patriarchal societies, where male and female roles are sharply distinguished and women have a passive role, that in fantasy produce myths of a female savior." In fantasy, the danger woman poses to the status quo is limited. Woman does in myth what she cannot do in the real world.

[22]On the use of "female" rather than "woman" (gynē) cf. 9:10, 13:15, 16:5; Craven, Artistry, 91 and n. 40; and esp. P.W. Skehan, "The Hand of Judith," CBQ 25 (1963) 94-109.

[23]Judith's appropriation of Holofernes's sword is to be equated not only with her assumption of male markers but also with castration. Castration is suggested also by Judith's comparison in 16:7 to figures who castrate their fathers: the young men, the sons of the Titans, and the giants in 16:7. Judith, like Medusa the archetypal phallic woman, castrates with "the beauty of her countenance" (16:7e). Consequently, she must be disarmed, and her disarming presence must be removed from the public sphere.

[24]As observed by Roitman, "Achior in the Book of Judith."

ACHIOR IN THE BOOK OF JUDITH: HIS ROLE AND SIGNIFICANCE

Adolfo D. Roitman
Hebrew University, Jerusalem

The book of Judith is one of the most beautiful as well as controversial books in apocryphal literature. Except for the issue of the original language, on which there is a virtual consensus among scholars, [1] a serious controversy remains about most of the external aspects of the book, e.g., its date,[2] the place of its composition[3] and the author.[4]

The mystery involves not only the origin of the book but also its content. The book contains many historical and geographical contradictions or errors, inconsistencies and improbabilities,[5] which have troubled scholars and exegetes for centuries.[6]

The present paper should be considered as part of this broader concern with perplexing problems. Our study will focus on one of the greatest mysteries of the book: Achior the Ammonite.

Achior appears in both parts of the book.[7] His first appearance is in chap. 5 (Part I). Holofernes, the commander of the Assyrian forces, surprised by the resistance offered by the Jews of the city of Bethulia to his army, asks many questions about their nature (5:1-4) and Achior, the leader of the Ammonites, who had joined the Assyrian forces in order to take part in the destruction of Israel, comes forward to supply "the truth concerning this people" (v 5).[8] He does it by surveying the sacred history of Israel (5:6-19). His words, especially his recommendation to Holofernes (vv 20-21), do not please Holofernes and his generals (5:22-6:9). Consequently, he is expelled from the Assyrian encampment and left tied near the city of Bethulia (6:10-13). Subsequently, he is released by the Jews and brought into the city, where he tells what happened to him (vv 14-17). Finally, he is praised by the people, and Uzziah, one of the leaders of the town, takes him to his house (vv 20-21).

He appears again in 14:5-10 (Part II).[9] Here, he is summoned by Judith in order to identify the head of Holofernes which she brought back with her to Bethulia. Upon seeing the head and hearing "all which the God of Israel had wrought, he believed in God with all his heart and got the flesh of his foreskin circumcised and was added to the house of Israel unto this day" (14:10).

From this brief summary, a number of surprising elements emerge. Achior is the only secondary character in the story whose role is developed.[10] He knows the sacred history of Israel exceedingly well

31

despite being a pagan. He is ready to suffer for Israel's faith as a martyr even though he belongs to the people of Ammon, a traditional enemy of the Jews.[11] And, most surprising of all, this Ammonite converts to Judaism.[12] Who indeed is Achior? How is one to account for these curious aspects of his role? What is his function in the story? Does he have any concealed significance?

Oddly enough, few scholars have dealt with the figure of Achior and attempted to resolve, even partially, the problems he presents. For example, although H. Cazelles[13] as well as J. Steinmann[14] clarified some obscure aspects of Achior, they fail to see his overall complex function and to integrate it into the structural framework of the story.

An important breakthrough on the subject is made by C. Moore:

> ...Achior is a crucial character for uniting both sections of the book. For Achior has one foot solidly planted in the first part (chaps. 5-6) and his second foot resting in the other (11:9-19; 14:6-10). Achior is a splendid study in contrasts and an effective foil for several of the book's characters. For example, in comparison to the wicked Holofernes, Achior is "the Righteous Gentile" who was saved by the Jews....When compared with Judith, Achior is the honest but ineffective advisor. An experienced soldier, Achior fainted when he saw the head that Judith had cut off with her own two hands. Yet Achior had more faith in the character and ways of Israel's God than did the magistrates of Bethulia.[15]

Nevertheless, even Moore does not pay attention to the fact that there is an especially intriguing structural relationship and a subtle complementarity between Achior and Judith which must be explained.[16]

The study consists of two parts. The first deals with the description of Achior's and Judith's respective functions. This is done by breaking up the appearances of both characters in the course of the story into five stages, and by pointing up in each of them their parallel or opposite construction and/or complementarity. The second part presents the explanation of the findings and the conclusion.

I. Description of the Functions of Achior and Judith
First Stage: Opposite Roles and Location

To begin with, Achior and Judith are thematically and functionally completely different. It is obvious from the information given about Achior in chap. 5 that he is a man, more specifically, the leader (ho hēgoumenos)[17] of the Ammonites, who had joined the army of Holofernes as a soldier so as to take part in the destruction of Israel. It is not clearly stated that he is a pagan, although it is taken for granted by the author.[18] His first appearance in the story is at the encampment of the Assyrians.

Judith, on the other hand, is described in contrast with Achior in full detail (8:1-8).[19] It is stated that this Israelite woman,[20] more specifically a widow (v 4), maintains a secluded way of life, removed from public affairs (vv 5-6). She is described as particularly beautiful, rich and pious (vv 7-8). Her first appearance is at the city of Bethulia.

Second Stage: Parallel Roles and Processes

Both characters, who in the first phase of the story stand in total opposition, show a startling similarity on a structural level in the second stage. There are all kinds of thematic and functional symmetries between them, either identities or antitheses.[21] Likewise, Achior and Judith undergo in this stage a basic change in their fundamental traits. These changes are essential for their later roles.

Achior delivers a speech (5:5-21) in which he gives Holofernes the information requested by him about the nature of the inhabitants of the city of Bethulia. Its content is largely a review of the sacred history of the Jews (vv 6-19). At the center of his speech, there stands a spiritual lesson as seen "by an outsider":[22] "And whilst they [i.e., the Jews] did not sin before their God, good things were theirs because God who hates iniquity was with them. But when they strayed from the path which He had appointed for them, they were utterly destroyed in many wars...." (vv 17-18ab). He ends his speech with a suggestion/advice (vv 20-21). Although he flatters Holofernes by such words as "thy slave" (v 5) and "most sovereign lord" (vv 20-21), his words arouse the anger of the Assyrian commander and his generals (5:22; 6:2). Surely, they feel that Achior has undergone a kind of transformation in the course of this speech -- from a pagan Ammonite at its beginning, to speaking like a "Jew" at its end.[23]

Having heard of the people's protest against Uzziah and the oath taken by him (8:9), Judith summons the elders of the city in order to deliver a speech to them (8:11-27).[24] First, she criticizes them very strongly (vv 11-16), and subsequently she suggests to them to wait for God's deliverance and to call upon Him for assistance (v 17). She supports her proposal by recalling the sacred history of Israel (vv 18-19). From that history a spiritual lesson as seen "by an insider" emerges: "But as for us, we have known no other God save Him; whence we hope that He will not despise us or any of our people" (v 20). She ends her speech with a recommendation (vv 24-25) based again on the lessons of the past (vv 26-27). Though she criticizes the elders of Bethulia, her words arouse excitement and wonder (vv 28-29). At the end of this stage, it is evident that Judith like Achior has undergone a notable change during and just after her speech -- beginning as a non-active, secluded and pious widow, at the end she has become a "heroine" (vv 32-34) and a "sensual woman" (10:3-4) -- so as to save Bethulia from destruction.[25]

Third Stage: Change of Places

In this phase, both characters change their locale in an inverted way.[26] This is a clever literary device used by the author not only in order to move the plot forward, but also and especially to complete the incipient transformation of Achior/Judith at the end of the last stage.

Achior, whom we first meet at the encampment of the Assyrians, is expelled by Holofernes and left tied near the city of Bethulia (6:7-13). Later, he is released by the Jews and brought (apēgagon) into the town and taken into the presence of the rulers of the city (6:14).

Judith, whom we first meet at the city of Bethulia, leaves it voluntarily (10:6-10). Afterwards, she is met by the Assyrians and brought (ēgagon) into the presence of Holofernes to whom she does obeisance (10:11-23).[27]

Fourth Stage: Change of Roles

Here both characters accomplish in their new surroundings their radical transformation initiated at the end of the second stage. However, the result is somewhat paradoxical. Once again, they play totally opposite roles, but unlike the first stage, in a reversed way.

Now Achior, heretofore the pagan soldier and enemy of Israel, appears as a betrayer of Holofernes (6:17) and a peaceful friend of the Jews in the city of Bethulia (6:20-21), while Judith, heretofore the secluded and pious Jewish widow, becomes a "liar" (e.g., 11:11-14), a "betrayer" (10:13; 11:16-19), and a "mistress" (12:15-19). And most extraordinary of all, she behaves like a "brave soldier" (13:6-8) in the encampment of the Assyrians.[28] It would seem that Achior plays, as it were, Judith's role in his new place, while Judith takes on Achior's.

However, this opposition is a fictitious one. Strictly speaking, only Achior has changed his fundamental traits, while Judith has undergone a pseudo-transformation in order to deceive Holofernes.

Even though they play "opposite roles," from a structural point of view Achior and Judith function in the same way in their new environment and elicit the same reactions from their hearers. Achior discloses Holofernes' plans to the inhabitants of Bethulia (6:17).[29] In consequence of this, he is highly praised by the people and is brought to Uzziah's house (6:20-21). Judith, on the other hand, reveals "Israel's plans" to Holofernes (11:11-14). Like Achior, she pleases the Assyrians (11:20-23), and is invited to stay at the encampment (12:1-4).

Many elements of Judith's speech to Holofernes (11:5-19) resemble very much aspects of Achior's address:

Achior/Holofernes

1. At their first encounter, Achior delivers a speech to Holofernes (5:5-21) in answer to the latter's questions (5:2-4);

2. He opens his speech with words stressing truth (5:5);[30]

3. His advice to Holofernes (5:20-21), in the light of the development of the story, is completely truthful;

4. Achior's speech is regarded by Holofernes as a prophecy (6:2);[31]

5. Holofernes' (6:2) and his generals' (5:22) reaction is highly negative.

Judith/Holofernes

1. At their first encounter, Judith delivers a speech to Holofernes (11:5-19) in answer to his question (11:3);
2. She opens her speech with words stressing truth (11:5);[32]
3. Her advice to Holofernes (11:17-19), in the light of the development of the story, is totally misleading;
4. Judith presents herself as a "prophetess" (11:16-19);[33]
5. Holofernes' and his people's reaction is highly positive (11:20).[34]

Fifth Stage: Meeting and Transformation of the Characters

In spite of the thematic and functional symmetries between the two characters in the narrative, their first encounter takes place almost at the very end of the story (14:6-10).[35] Theoretically, they could have met before.[36] Although Judith knows about Achior (11:9), the author did not want them to meet until this point in the story.

Having killed Holofernes, Judith comes back to Bethulia (13:10-13). Upon returning to the Jewish town she does not immediately resume her previous status but for a while plays the role of a commander (14:1-4). It is at the peak of this role-playing that she finally meets Achior.[37] This is accomplished by summoning Achior to identify the head of Holofernes (14:5).[38]

At this meeting, Achior does two things. First, he recognizes the superiority of Judith: "...he fell at Judith's feet and did obeisance unto her (prosekunēsen tō prosōpō autēs)[39] and said, "Blessed shalt thou be in every tent of Judah, and in every nation those who hear thy name will be terror-struck" (v 7). Second, he completes his radical transformation begun in the second and fourth stage. At the beginning he is a leader and a soldier. Now, at the end of the tale, he behaves like a civilian. When Achior sees the head of Holofernes "he fell upon his face and became as one dead" (14:6) as if it were the first time in his life he had seen this kind of thing.[40] Moreover, at the beginning he is a pagan Ammonite, but after hearing "all which the God of Israel had wrought, he believed in God with all his heart[41] and got the flesh of his foreskin circumcised and was added to the house of Israel unto this day" (v 10). After this conversion,[42] Achior does not appear again.

On the other hand, Judith gradually resumes her former conduct after the meeting with Achior and the defeat of the Assyrians (15:1-7): first, her piety (15:14-16:19); after that, her retirement (v 21); and finally, her widow's weeds (v 22).[43]

Now, let us summarize the above-mentioned details in a table in order to present them clearly before proceeding to the second part.

ACHIOR	JUDITH

-First Stage: Opposite Roles and Location-

Man (5:5)	Beautiful woman (8:7)
Ammonite/enemy of Israel (5:5)	Israelite (8:1)
Leader and soldier (5:5)	Secluded widow (8:4-6)
Pagan	Believer in God (8:8)
Encampment of the Assyrians	City of Bethulia

-Second Stage: Parallel Roles and Processes-

Delivery of a speech (5:5-21)	Delivery of a speech (8:11-27)
history of the Jews (5:6-19)	history of the Jews (8:18-19, 26-27)
spiritual lesson (5:17-18ab)	spiritual lesson (8:20)
suggestion/advice (5:20-21)	suggestion/recommendation (8:17, 24-25)
flattering words (5:5, 20-21)	criticism (8:11-16)
Anger as reaction (5:22; 6:2)	Wonder as reaction (8:28-29)
Transformation into a "Jew"	Transformation into a "heroine" (8:32-34) and a "sensual woman" (10:3-4)

-Third State: Change of Places-

Expelled from the Assyrian encampment (6:7-13)	Left Bethulia voluntarily (10:6-10)
Brought into Bethulia and taken into the presence of the rulers of the city (6:14)	Brought into the presence of Holofernes (10:11-23)

-Fourth Stage: Change of Roles-

Betrayer of Holofernes (6:17)	"Liar" (e.g., 11:11-15); "betrayer" (11:16-19); "mistress" (12:13-19)
Peaceful friend of the Jews (6:20-21)	"Brave soldier" (13:3-8)

Function and Reactions

Disclosure of Holofernes' plans (6:17)	Disclosure of "Israel's plans" (11:11-14)
Praised by the people and brought to Uzziah's house (6:20-21)	Praised by the people (11:20-23) and invited to stay at the encampment (12:5)

Speech

A speech (5:5-21) in answer to Holofernes' questions (5:2-4)	A speech (11:5-19) in answer to Holofernes' question (11:3)
Opening words stressing truth (5:5)	Opening words stressing truth (11:5)
Truthful advice (5:20-21)	Misleading advice (11:17-19)
Speech is regarded as a prophecy (6:2)	Judith as "prophetess" (11:17-19)
Negative reaction of Holofernes and his people (5:22, 6:2)	Positive reaction of Holofernes and his people (11:20-23)

-Fifth Stage: Meeting and Transformation of the Characters-

Meeting with Judith (14:6-10)	Commander role (14:1-4)
Transformation into a civilian (14:6) and a Jew (14:10)	Transformation into a pious (15:14-16:19) and secluded widow (16:21-22)

II. Explanation and Conclusion

The first part of this paper sought to demonstrate that Achior is much more than "un personnage episodique,"[44] or "a splendid study in contrasts and an effective foil for several of the book's characters."[45] He is designed thematically as well as functionally as the mirror image of Judith, being a kind of double or "alter ego." In some way, the Ammonite leader is the masculine/pagan version of the feminine/Jewish Judith.

What has been said above is true till virtually the end of the narrative when both characters meet one another for the first time. Here, the thematic and functional similarity and/or complementarity between

Judith and her double reaches a resolution.[46] Since the motif of widowhood is highly important in the book,[47] the writer did not want to resolve the tension by having them marry each other. Therefore, the only way he could find to break the equilibrium was to blur the last two essential differences between the two, viz., by converting Achior into a civilian and a Jew, and thus bringing him as close as possible to Judith.

But if this analysis is correct, one faces a serious question: Why did the author portray Achior who is a soldier and pagan Ammonite as the thematic and functional counterbalance of Judith, the Jewish heroine of the book? It may have been done for purely literary reasons. Or was it because the unknown writer is trying to tell us something through this literary device?

Obviously, no definitive answer to this question is possible. Nevertheless, it could be said that Achior's role in the story might be understood as a result of the ideology of proselytism that underlies the national, almost nationalistic, atmosphere of the book.[48] The author wanted, presumably, to teach us through this very sophisticated technique that a righteous pagan, even one who belongs to the hateful people of Ammon, is, essentially, the parallel and complement to a complete Jew by birth, and that he is able to perfect his condition by believing in God and joining the people of Israel through conversion. However, it must be taken into account that this stance is not, as it has been argued, "presque évangélique,"[49] but has a nationalistic undertone. His conversion is meant to prove the main thesis of the book: the superiority of the Jews and their beliefs over the world of the pagans.

This subtle ideology of proselytism might also explain the literary fact that the traditions about Abraham (5:6-9) function as a model for both Judith and Achior.[50] Abraham is described in this brief section as a great believer who is ready to suffer for his faith, and who stands in contrast to the pagan Chaldeans as well as to the Exodus generation.[51] His attitude anticipates Judith's. Judith like Abraham is described as a great believer in God, who denies the divinity of Nebuchadnezzar, and who fiercely opposes the pagans. Yet Judith also stands in contrast to the Jews of Bethulia. While she has a strong faith in God and is willing to suffer for it (8:24-27), the Jews of Bethulia were ready to surrender to the Assyrian army (7:23-28). Likewise, Abraham is also the model for Achior. Both (1) believe in God (5:8ab//14:10), (2) are expelled because of their faith (5:8c//6:11), and (3) convert to a new faith (5:8ab//14:10).[52] A linguistic parallel between Achior and Abraham can also be adduced. It is said of Achior in 14:10 that he "believed in God" (episteusen tō theō).[53] Strikingly enough, the same expression appears only once throughout the entire Bible in Gen 15:6 to describe Abraham's belief in God (wh'myn byhwh = episteusen tō theō [LXX]).[54]

That is to say, according to the book of Judith, the righteous pagan who converts to Judaism would also have, as the native Jew has, Abraham as his model or "father." Such a doctrine strongly resembles the teachings of Philo[55] and the rabbis[56] some centuries later.

To sum up, our present paper has attempted to demonstrate that Achior is a very skillfully crafted character. He is described thematically as well as functionally throughout the narrative as the mirror image of Judith, being a kind of double or "alter ego." This role could be understood as the literary expression of the ideology of proselytism that underlies the book.[57]

---

[1]It is agreed that there was originally a Hebrew Vorlage. However, it has been argued recently by T. Craven that Judith could have been composed from the outset in an "elegant hebraicised Greek" (Artistry and Faith in the Book of Judith [SBLDS 70; Chico: Scholars Press, 1983] 5). The text is extant in Greek (LXX) and in many other translations (Latin, Syriac, Coptic, Ethiopic and Armenian). There are also at least five medieval Hebrew texts. On all these matters, see C. Moore, Judith (AB 40; Garden City, NY: Doubleday, 1985) 66-67, 91-108.

[2]The various theories may be classified into three categories: 1. "Persian period" (J. Grintz, The Book of Judith [Jerusalem: Mosad Bialik, 1957; reprinted 1986] 3-55 [Hebrew]); 2. "Two-stages composition" - the first composition in the Persian period and the rewriting of it in the Hellenistic period - (G.W.E. Nickelsburg, "Stories of Biblical and Early Post-Biblical Times" in M. Stone, ed., Jewish Writings of the Second Temple Period [CRINT 2/2; Assen/Philadelphia: Van Gorcum/Fortress Press, 1984] 51; J.C. Greenfield, "The Jewish Historical Novel in the Persian Period," in H. Tadmor and I. Ephal, eds., The History of the People of Israel [Jerusalem: Am Oved, 1983] 209 [Hebrew]); 3. "Hasmonean period" (P. Winter, "Judith, Book of," IDB 2.1025; O. Eissfeldt, The Old Testament: An Introduction [Oxford: Basil Blackwell, 1974] 587; E. Schürer, The History of the Jewish People in the Age of Jesus Christ [175 B.C. - A.D. 135] [3/1 ed. and rev. by G. Vermes, F. Millar and M. Goodman; Edinburgh: T. & T. Clark, 1986] 218-219; Moore, Judith, 67-70; M. Enslin and S. Zeitlin, The Book of Judith [Leiden: Brill, 1972] 26-31).

[3]For example, Antioch (Zeitlin, Judith, 31-32; B.Z. Lurie, "Jews of Syria in the Days of Antiochus Epiphanes and the Book of Judith," Bet Miqra 62 [1975] 328-341 [Hebrew]) or Palestine (Moore, Judith, 70-71).

[4]E.g., a Pharisee (Moore, ibid.) or a Sadducee (H. Mantel, "Ancient Sadducean Piety" in Mantel, The Men of the Great Synagogue [Tel Aviv: Dvir, 1983] 134-145 [Hebrew]). According to Craven's opinion (Artistry and Faith 121), "there is in fact no reason to believe that either a Sadducee, a Zealot, an Essene, or a Pharisee authored the story."

[5]See many examples in Moore, Judith, 46-49, and in J. Licht, "The Book of Judith as a Literary Work," Sefer Baruch Kurzweil (ed. A. Saltman, et.al.; Tel Aviv: Shogan, 1975) 170-172 (Hebrew).

[6]Most recently, it has been proposed that irony could be the "key" to the eccentricities of the book. On this see Moore, Judith, 78-85.

[7]The book is usually divided into two parts: Part I (chaps. 1-7) and Part II (chaps. 8-16). On the structure of the book, see Craven, Artistry and Faith, 47-64.

[8]All the quotations follow, unless otherwise noted, the translation of Enslin, Book of Judith.

[9]In 11:9-10 Achior is only mentioned by Judith as the background for her speech to Holofernes.

[10]Cf. Licht, "The Book of Judith," 179.

[11]Cf. 1 Samuel 11; Amos 1:13-14; Jer 49:1-6; Ezek 25:1-7; etc. On the biblical stance towards the Ammonites see Encyclopaedia Biblica, s.v. "Ammon," 6.269-270 (Hebrew). It is all the more unusual if we take into consideration that the Jews of Bethulia were ready to surrender to the Assyrians; see 7:23-28.

[12]For some scholars (see, for example, Moore, Judith, 235-236; Grintz, Book of Judith, 45; Nickelsburg, "Stories," 49, Zeitlin, Judith, 24-25), Achior's conversion to Judaism is an astonishing detail since it would appear to be in direct contradiction to Deut 23:4: "No Ammonite or Moabite is to be admitted to the assembly of Yahweh; not even their descendants to the tenth generation may be admitted to the assembly of Yahweh, and this is for all time." (The biblical texts are quoted according to JB.) This is so because they understand the words in Deuteronomy "to be admitted to the assembly of Yahweh" in a quite literal sense, that is to say: "to join the Israelites" or, in other words, "to convert." Actually, as Shaye J.D. Cohen shows ("From the Bible to the Talmud: The Prohibition of Intermarriage" HAR 7 [1983] 33), this understanding can already be found in Philo and in the Church Fathers (Clement of Alexandria, Tertullian and Origen). But, it is not altogether sure that this was the most common way people understood the expression in antiquity. There existed in ancient Israel two other interpretations of the verse. Besides that of Philo, Cohen says, the rabbis in the Mishnah and Talmud assumed that all the pericope in which our verse appears (Deut 23:2-9) speaks about forbidden marriages (cf. m. Qidd. 4:3). Likewise, an alternative understanding was that "to be admitted to the assembly of Yahweh" means "to be admitted into the temple and/or holy city" (for example, Lam 1:10; 4Q Florilegium; Temple Scroll; etc.). Prof. Cohen may be quite right when he concludes that "the author of Judith...did not understand Deut 23:4 in Philonic fashion, because he narrates, without the least sign of disapproval, the circumcision and conversion of Achior, an Ammonite general" (ibid., 33). Nevertheless, even if the widely-accepted "legal" contradiction in Achior's conversion were not an intentional one forged by the author but, most probably, due to a misunderstanding of

the scholars, at any rate a striking element remains: Why did the author choose precisely a socially undersirable Ammonite as a convert to Judaism?

[13]He argues that Achior is used by the author as a type "pour communiquer à leurs lecteurs un développement théologique sur le rôle de la justice et l'élection des Gentiles" ("Le personnage d'Achior dans le livre de Judith," RSR 39 [1951] 134). Also, he dwells largely in his article on the origin of the character. He maintains that Achior the Ammonite is a new ethnic transformation of the ancient and famous Assyrian sage Ahikar, from whom he inherited his central feature -- that of being a good and righteous pagan who is persecuted by evil powers. The "Ahikar theory" has been accepted by Moore (Judith, 163) and E. Haag (Studien zum Buche Judith: Seine theologische Bedeutung und literarisches Eigenart [Trierer Theologische Studien 16; Trier: Paulinus-Verlag, 1963] 32-33), but strongly rejected by J. Steinmann ("Achior, prosélyte et prophète" [in Steinmann, Lecture de Judith [Paris: J. Gabalda, 1953] 55) and Grintz, (Book of Judith, 110).

[14]He makes some important observations on the function of Achior in chap. 5 as a "prophet" and "proselyte," and on the opposition Achior/Uzziah. See "Achior," 55-62.

[15]Judith, 59. Cf. also Licht, "The Book of Judith," 177.

[16]Scholars have alrady noted the thematic relationship between Judith and Holofernes, (e.g., T. Craven, "Artistry and Faith in the Book of Judith," Semeia 8 [1977] 93), but as far as I know, this is the first time that the relationship between Judith and Achior is emphasized.

[17]All the quotations in Greek follow, unless otherwise noted, the Cambridge edition (Alan Brooke, Norman McLean and H. St. John Thackeray, editors, Esther, Judith, Tobit: The Old Testament in Greek, 3.1 (London: Cambridge University Press, 1940).

[18]If not, his conversion at the end (14:10) would be senseless.

[19]Actually, this is the only description of a character in the narrative. Undoubtedly, this is because Judith is the pivotal character in the book.

[20]The contrast man/woman is not an artificial one, but an essential tension in the story. It is not accidental that the males are the principal characters of Part I, while a female, Judith, plays the principal role in Part II.

[21]On this literary feature in the book, see Craven, Artistry and Faith, 53-59.

[22]For Licht's distinction between Achior's spiritual lesson and Judith's (cf. below), see "The Book of Judith," 177.

[23]This is so because Achior does not behave according to the pagan's stereotype.

[24]This action is already a change in her previous tendency to self-seclusion and lack of involvement in public affairs; see 8:4. Also notable is the fact that this public appearance of Judith and her speech contradicts some stereotypes of a woman's function in ancient society. Cf. Philo, Spec. Leg. 3.171. On a woman's role in ancient Jewish society see Theodore Friedman, "The Shifting Role of Women, from the Bible to Talmud," Judaism

36 (1987) 479-487.

[25]Again, this attitude stands against the cultural stereotype. For example, Philo says:
> And so in wars and campaigns and emergencies which threaten the whole country they [i.e., women] are not allowed to take their place according to the judgement of the law, having in view the fitness of things, which it was resolved to keep unshaken always and everywhere and considered to be in itself more valuable than victory or liberty or success of any kind.

(Spec. Leg. 3.172; Translation of F.H. Colson and G.H. Whitaker, Philo [10 vols.; LCL, Cambridge: Harvard/London: Heinemann, 1929-62] 7.583).

[26]It is important to bear in mind that Achior and Judith are the only two central characters in the story who do this. Nevertheless, there is a great difference between them. On the one hand, Achior is carried to Bethulia and definitely remains there. On the other, Judith makes a double exchange: she leaves Bethulia temporarily and comes to the Assyrians' encampment, but afterwards she departs from there and returns to her city.

[27]From a structural point of view, the coming of Judith to the Assyrian encampment makes it possible to maintain the balance of the two locales. The encampment of the Assyrians had expelled one person (Achior) and the city of Bethulia gained a new inhabitant. Therefore, it was necessary for literary reasons to regain the balance between the two places by removing one character from the Jewish town (Judith) and placing her in the Assyrian encampment.

[28]About this role see above n. 25. However, this behavior recalls strongly Jael's (Judg 4:17-21).

[29]The appearances of Achior are, from a functional point of view, essential for the development of the story. As a result of his speech (5:5-21) Holofernes issues an order to wage war against the children of Israel (7:1-7), while after he disclosed Holofernes' plans to the inhabitants of Bethulia Judith made her appearance as "the Savior" (chap. 8).

[30]"I will tell thee the truth (anaggelō soi tēn alētheian);" "no lie shall come forth (ouk exeleusetai pseudos) from the mouth of my slave."

[31]On the function of Achior as prophet in chap. 5 see Steinmann, "Achior," 56. On the relationship between Balaam "the prophet" and Achior see Moore, Judith, 166.

[32]"I will tell my lord nothing false (ouk anaggelō pseudos)." Cf. 10:13.

[33]This adduced "attribute" of Judith along with the above-mentioned traits of her widowhood (8:4-5) and piety (fast [8:6]; prayer [9; 12:6, etc.]; and ablutions [12:7]) recall in a very suggestive way Anna's characteristics in Luke: "There was a prophetess also, Anna the daughter of Phanuel, of the tribe of Asher. She was well on in years. Her days of girlhood over, she had been married for seven years before becoming a widow. She was now eighty-four years old and never left the Temple, serving God night and day with fasting and prayer."(2:36-37) It is not unreasonable to suppose, then, that the author took his inspiration for characterizing Judith from real pious widows who existed in Second Temple society.

[34]This fact is a result of the implicit irony of the narrative. See Moore, Judith, 83.

[35]This is in accordance with the author's technique by which he resolves in the second part of the story situations constructed in the first, such as: the siege of Bethulia by the Assyrians/the defeat of the Assyrians by the Jews; the boasting of Holofernes/the killing of Holofernes, etc.

[36]For example, between the coming of Achior to Bethulia (6:14) and the departure of Judith from the city (10:6).

[37]Some scholars believe that 14:5-10 is intrusive and that the sequence in the Vulgate (i.e., before Judith outlined the battle strategy for the next day) would be much better. Cf. Moore, Judith, 234. My opinion is that this approach fails to appreciate the blatant irony of this whole scene.

[38]He was the only person in Bethulia who could testify as to the identity of the head.

[39]Note the ironical contrast between Achior's sincere submission to Judith and Judith's hypocritical yielding to Holofernes ("and falling upon her face she did obeisance to him" [kai pesousa epi prosōpon prosekunēsen autǭ; 10:23]).

[40]The ironical contrast between Judith's commander-soldier role and Achior's civilian and less macho role is apparent.

[41]Grintz (Book of Judith, 167) errs when he identifies Achior's reaction with the traditional biblical motif of "the recognition of the greatness of God by a Gentile" (see, Exod 18:1-11 [Jethro]; Josh 2:9-11 [Rahab]; 1 Kgs 5:21 [Hiram]; 10:9 [Queen of Sheba]; 2 Kgs 5:15 [Naaman]; Dan 3:28-32 [Nebuchadnezzar]; 6:26-28 [Darius] etc.). According to S.J.D. Cohen ("Crossing the Boundary and Becoming a Jew" HTR 82 [1989] 17), the gentiles of the last category "do not stand in any special relationship with the God of the Jews. They behave as 'normal' pagans behave when confronted by a foreign god and foreign religion." Achior, on the other hand, not only "recognizes the greatness of God" but also converts to Judaism. On Achior's belief in God cf. also nn. 53 and 54.

[42]"Here we clearly see conversion for the first time [in Jewish history]: belief in the true God accompanied by circumcision and a change in identity" (Cohen, "Conversion to Judaism in Historical Perspective: From Biblical Israel to Post-Biblical Judaism," Conservative Judaism 36 [1983] 35). Cf. also n. 12. Interestingly, the development of Achior in the book -- from a righteous pagan to a convert -- recalls the progress undergone by Rahab in ancient Jewish literature. This harlot, who is pictured in the book of Joshua as a righteous pagan who recognizes that "Yahweh your God is both in heaven above and on earth beneath" (2:11), becomes in rabbinic literature a pious convert (cf. Num. Rab. 8 [end], etc.).

[43]However, it must be noted that the resumption is not absolute. Cf. 8:4-6.

[44]Cazelles, "Achior," 134.

[45]Moore, Judith, 59. Cf. also Licht, "Book of Judith," 177.

[46]For this reason, the author did not bring them together before this.

[47]Cf. 8:4-5; 16:22. About "widowhood" as a literary motif and as a religious value, see P. Sandevoir, "Viudas" in Vocabulario de Teología Bíblica (ed. X. Leon-Dufour; Barcelona: Ed. Herder, 1980) 961-962.

[48]Cazelles, ("Achior," 134, 137) and Steinmann ("Achior," 62) also paid attention to the "universal trend" that underlies Judith. Moore criticizes this understanding by pointing to the fact that "...if so, such tender and compassionate feelings toward non-Jews is observable nowhere else in Judith" (Judith, 235). Actually, the conclusion should be the contrary. Precisely in the light of the fact that Achior's conversion is the only expression of "universalism" that appears in the book, it should be considered doubly significant.

[49]Steinmann, "Achior," 62. Cf. Cazelles, "Achior," 134.

[50]This finding indirectly confirms our thesis of the parallelism and complementarity between them. On Abraham traditions in Judith see my article "The Traditions about Abraham's Early Life in the Book of Judith" (forthcoming).

[51]The opposition between Abraham and the pagan Chaldeans is obvious; see 5:8. The contrast between Abraham and the Exodus generation is more subtle. If we compare the Abraham section (5:6-9) with the Exodus-generation section (vv 10-14a), which appears in the same literary context of Achior's speech (5:5-21), it can be seen that the author seeks to demonstrate the superiority of Abraham's faith. I hope to prove this statement in a forthcoming paper.

[52]We have to bear in mind that the traditions about Abraham are contained in Achior's own speech. He opens his review of Israel's sacred history with a description of Abraham as the first "convert" at 5:6-9 (Part I), while he closes the circle when he converts to Abraham's faith in 14:10 (Part II). On this technique in the book, see above n. 35.

[53]The belief of a gentile in God is very uncommon in the Bible. The only known parallel for this is Jon 3:5.

[54]I thank Prof. D. Dimant for having called my attention to this fact. It is suggestive that Gen 15:6 played a key role in Abraham's evaluation in Judaism (cf. Sir 44:20; 1 Macc 2:52; Jub 17:17-18) and in Christianity, especially in Paul's proselytizing of gentiles (cf. Gal 3:6-14; Rom 4:1-25)!! See also Jas 2:23.

[55]Cf. Virt. 219. About his teachings, see J.S. Bosch, "La figura de Abrahán en Pablo y en Filón de Alejandría" in Salvación de la Palabra. Targum-Derash-Berith. En memoria del Profesor Alejandro Diez Macho (ed. D. M. Leon; Madrid: Ed. Cristiandad; 1986) 677-688, esp. 687.

[56]See C.G. Montefiore and H. Loewe, A Rabbinic Anthology (New York: Schocken Books, 1974) 574 (1599), 577-578 (1608).

[57]I am grateful to the Memorial Foundation for Jewish Culture and the Wharburg Prize (Hebrew University) for the financial assistance given to me in order to pursue this research. I owe my thanks, also, to Prof. M.E. Stone, Prof. S.J.D. Cohen, Dr. D.R. Schwartz and Rabbi Dr. T. Friedman for their assistance and comments.

JUDITH, HOLDING THE TALE OF HERODOTUS
Mark Stephen Caponigro

Is the Book of Judith in part modeled on Herodotus' account of the Persian invasions of Greece in the fifth century B.C.E.? Was the author of Judith acquainted with the Histories? The idea is by no means a new one; and most students of Judith seem not to find it very interesting.[1] But if it should ever come to be seen as not only interesting but even probably correct, it would alter our appreciation of Judith, its author, and its genre. No less important, it would offer another curious detail to complicate further our already very complicated ideas about Hellenistic Jewish culture.

What follows is an attempt to argue that the author of Judith (henceforth to be called "the Auctrix") did indeed have some acquaintance with the Histories of Herodotus, and borrowed from them something of their narrative structure, as well as certain specific narrative elements, for use in her own post-biblical, fictional history/hagiography.[2] The argument is based on the observation that several places in the Septuagint text of Judith, in themselves difficult to understand, become much more explicable when they are recognized to be less than perfectly coherent adaptations of Herodotean material to a new and different story.

It should be established at once that similarities between Judith and Herodotus, no matter how close or how numerous, are in themselves useless for the purpose of this argument. If a feature in Judith reminds us of something in Herodotus, but on the other hand can be thought reasonably to have an independent, non-Herodotean origin, then it does not help us at all in affirming a Judith/Herodotus connection.

So for example, the basic international predicaments in Judith and Herodotus are strikingly similar: The ruler of a mighty empire in the East, a monarch of overweening and tyrannical complexion, sends a great and terrible host against some smaller states to the West, to punish them for somehow offending him; the invading force is frightfully destructive; some of the westerners are overrun; others capitulate, which the reader is urged to consider shameful; but still others, the heroes, resist, and are able first to embarrass the invader, and at last to defeat him decisively; the victory is attributed in large measure to the rare or even super-human virtues of the defenders, especially those of a few remarkable individuals who emerge to lead the defense, and also in part to divine assistance. But none of this is useful. This outline of an invasion story, common to Judith and Herodotus, looks long and complex enough nearly to force the conclusion that the later writer got it from the earlier. In fact, however, every item in the outline can be found as well in biblical literature and the history of Israel. No Judith/Herodotus connection can be persuasively affirmed on this basis.

Then there is this: In both narratives the leader of the invading army receives a warning that points out how difficult it will be to defeat the defenders holding out against him, on account of some terrific virtue that they have; he does not heed the warning, and in the ensuing conflict the terrific virtue of the defenders is made manifest. Xerxes, the second of Herodotus' royal invaders, in fact has two such counsellors: his uncle Artabanus, who praises the Athenians and preaches about divine justice that strikes down the lofty (Hist. vii.10) at the outset of the campaign; and Demaratus, the deposed king of Sparta, who answers Xerxes' questions about the likelihood of Greek resistance by warning him not to attack the Spartans at Thermopylae (vii.101-104). In Judith the discouraging counsellor is Achior (5:5-21). Both he and Artabanus receive angry replies to their words, and both suffer as a result a kind of banishment, more brutal in the case of Achior. By contrast, Demaratus' no less discouraging advice provokes laughter in the king. Momigliano, however, was especially impressed by how Demaratus' analysis of Spartan military prowess, directly dependent on the Spartans' obedience to nomos, "Law," resembles what Achior says about the Israelites, declaring them invincible provided they avoid sinning against their God (5:17, 20-21).

But this gets us nowhere. Achior in fact says nothing specifically about Torah, even when he is talking about the Exodus and Sinai. And more generally, his message is quite at home in biblical literature, sounding something very like the Deuteronomic theory of Israelite history. Also he himself, saying what he does at this point in the story, plays a role like that of the Gentile prophet Balaam (cf. Numbers 22-24, especially the angry reaction of Balak at 24:10-11; and the use of the verb prophesy in Jdt 6:2). Once again what seemed like solid evidence for Herodotean influence on Judith turns out to be problematic.

There are however other places in Judith that are clearly reminiscent of Herodotean material, and, besides, have no apparent origin in biblical literature or Israelite history. Moreover they are not in themselves very easy to understand; they show the signs of strain and forcing, the introduction of something alien into a place where it does not belong and was not meant to be.

The first of these places is at Jdt 2:7, a detail in Nebuchadnezzar's orders to Holofernes: "And you will proclaim to them to have earth and water prepared." The Persian practice of demanding earth and water from foreign states as a sign of their submission to the Persian king is well known from Herodotus (vi.48; vi.94; vii.131ff). Where did the Auctrix learn of it? From Herodotus? Or from some other, non-Herodotean, quite possibly even non-Hellenic channel of information about Persian matters?

Before we answer, we should make a couple of observations. First, there is nothing in Judith that explains the point of preparing earth and water; there is nothing in the immediate context, and there are no other references to Nebuchadnezzar's demand elsewhere in the book. Apparently the Auctrix considered a demand for earth and water appropriate to the kind of speech Nebuchadnezzar is making, and not needing to be explained. How did the Auctrix' contemporary readers understand Nebuchadnezzar's demand? How would we understand it, if the relevant passages in Herodotus were not extant and we knew nothing of the Persian practice? As a metaphorical expression equivalent to a demand for the absolute surrender of all territory? Perhaps; but the purpose of the campaign is not really to conquer territory.

On the other hand, having Herodotus helps us only so far. Nebuchadnezzar's demand is in fact quite different from anything put on the lips of Darius or Xerxes. Herodotus makes a clear distinction: those states that indicate their submission by offering the earth and water will not be punished by the Persian king; those that do not submit, will be punished. Both invading kings seem to take the distinction seriously. Darius is glad to have an excuse to conquer the Greek cities that do not submit (vi.94); and Xerxes, who sent heralds after earth and water to many places in Greece (vii.131-132), makes a point of not sending any to Athens and Sparta, in part because the Athenians and Spartans mistreated the heralds of Darius (vii.133), but also no doubt because he wants to remain free to crush them. It is quite contrary to this pattern, then, and pointless too as a result, that Nebuchadnezzar demands earth and water from states that he intends to punish all the same.

Also, in Herodotus the protocol is simple and straight-forward: heralds are sent out to the state in question in advance of the king's army, make the demand, and return with or without the tokens of submission. (In Judith something like this may in fact be intended in Nebuchadnezzar's original message to the West during his campaign against the Medes. Otherwise the adjective "empty-handed," which is how his ambassadors are said to return to him in 1:11, is purely metaphorical.) But in Nebuchadnezzar's speech, the procedure becomes rather more complicated. Holofernes is charged to order the westerners to "have earth and water prepared"--whatever that may mean; it does not sound quite the same as giving earth and water to a herald, nor is Holofernes expected to carry it back to Nebuchadnezzar if it is offered. Then, in 2:10-11, Nebuchadnezzar distinguishes between those who surrender to Holofernes, and those who do not. Holofernes is to punish the latter harshly; the former he is to keep under guard until Nebuchadnezzar himself comes to punish them (cf. also 2:7b: "for I will go out in my wrath against them"). The purpose of the double punishment is less than clear. Holofernes seems to be given two quite separate, hardly compatible roles: one, that of the Herodotean earth-and-water herald, sent out in advance of a king who is sure to follow and take action upon the basis of the herald's report; the other, that of the agent chosen to go forth and himself carry out the will of the king, the king staying at home. (Hence also the difficulty of translating proerchesthai in 2:19. Is it "to go forth from," as translated above, or is it "to proceed ahead of"?)

We are left with two alternatives. 1. The Auctrix got the earth and water for 2:7 from a non-Herodotean source. In that case we must admit the possibility that the demand for earth and water was used in Persian diplomacy--and why now Persian?, why limit ourselves to that?--in ways quite unlike what Herodotus told us; and we must accept the coincidence that a narrative detail reminding us very strongly of something in Herodotus, but not in fact coming from there, should have dropped into a narrative that also happens to remind us of Herodotus. 2. The Auctrix got it from Herodotus. And in that case we have to cope with the curious differences discussed above.

But in fact this alternative is the easier. What seems to have happened is that the Auctrix, loosely following the outline of Herodotus' invasion narratives, wanted to include a reference to that element in the story which vividly recalls both the western heroes' bold defiance and the eastern despot's vengeful wrath. Is the incoherence of the introduced element a result of ineptitude or of art? Let us say, of art. The style of the Auctrix is learned and allusive, and also what we might call impressionistic, achieving its effect by a non-literal, history-resistant, even incoherent deployment of allusions. Well known examples are the startling association of names in 1:1, and the impossible chronology of 4:3. The names and historical events that appear in Judith do not signify themselves; rather, they signify what they felt like in the stories where the Auctrix first found them. She made from them her vocabulary, with which to tell a new story having nothing necessarily to do with the history or histories she had read. So one vocabulum in her lexicon is the demand for earth and water--by the way we observe that her sources and her allusions are not all biblical; with that she hoped to add the wrath of Darius and Xerxes, setting their faces against Greece, to her portrait of Nebuchadnezzar.

We seem to find another example of this stylistic feature at 2:1-3. The palace conference of the king with his servants and nobles does not recall any obvious biblical precedent. Moreover, it is not consistent with the characterization of the utterly autocratic and resolute Nebuchadnezzar established in chap. 1 (cf. especially 1:12). If 2:1-4a had been lost in a lacuna, it is doubtful that an editor would have supplied anything like it.

Again it is a question of Xerxizing the portrait of Nebuchadnezzar, in preparation for the subsequent Xerxish invasion. The relevant passage in Herodotus is vii.5-11. It begins with a speech by Mardonius urging Xerxes to invade Greece, and culminates in the conference of Persian nobles whose support for the campaign Xerxes seeks to elicit. A brief analysis will show how much this passage has in common with Jdt 2:1-3.

Neither an easy verse to understand nor to translate, Jdt 2:1 means literally something like this: "And in the eighteenth year, on the twenty-second day of the first month, there was talk, in the house of Nebuchadnezzar the king of the Assyrians, of punishing all the earth, as he had spoken."[3] There are at least two problems of interpretation here. First, the palace discourse seems not to come from the mouth of Nebuchadnezzar, but rather to be made by another, or by others, for his benefit; and that is inconsistent, as we observed, with what was established in the previous chapter, that the intention to punish the West was originally and particularly Nebuchadnezzar's, and was solemnly resolved upon (1:12). The narrative problem of how to bridge the gap between the victory celebration of 1:16 and the commission of Holofernes in 2:4-13 we might expect to have been solved by saying simply that the king remembered his oath and called up his general. Instead we get this curious indirect expression, which sounds almost as though the king needs to be reminded of his earlier resolve, or egged on to carry it out.

Secondly, just how is the "talk" related to Nebuchadnezzar's conference in 2:2-3? Some translators take "talk" to mean "deliberation" or "discussion," and treat it as a summary anticipation of the conference. But then the kai at the beginning of 2:2, which we would usually expect to set off a new and separate item, must be somehow overlooked, as though we had the license to consider it a not really meaningful Semitic particle placed there to help along the narrative flow.

Both these difficulties are clarified by recognizing that the Auctrix has inserted here a much compressed adaptation of the Herodotean passage mentioned above, vii.5-11. That passage too falls into two parts. The first, 5-7, tells of how Xerxes, originally not disposed to undertake a campaign against Greece, is persuaded to do so by Mardonius in the first place, then by some medizing Greek aristocrats. This is the model for Jdt 2:1. The second, 8-11, relates a different event, Xerxes' conference with the assembled Persian nobles. First he himself speaks, presenting his plan to invade and conquer Greece, and justifying it in large measure by recalling the wrongs committed by the Athenians for which they need to be punished. Then Mardonius responds, speaking in favor of the plan, and finally Artabanus, speaking against it, to the kings' displeasure, to which we referred above in a different context. Xerxes' convocation of the nobles and his speech to them form together the model for Jdt 2:2; Mardonius' speech is the model for 2:3. (The Auctrix chose not to use the speech of Artabanus here, but kept it in reserve. In fact she did use it later as one of the models for Achior's speech, though we were not ready to assert that when discussing the Achior passage above.)

It should be observed that in her adaptation of vii.5-7, the Auctrix kept her inconsistency minimal. The strangely impersonal expression, "there was talk of punishing as he had spoken," is in fact not really inconsistent with what we learned of Nebuchadnezzar's manner of expression, as well as of the unchallenged location of all authority in his person, chap. 1. On the other hand, it falls short of actually saying that he needs to be persuaded to carry out the very course of action that he resolved upon earlier, throwing rather a mist of obscurity around a palace loudly resounding with grave international threats.[4] As for Xerxes' conference, Herodotus is very interested, here as elsewhere, in presenting the delicacy of the Persian monarchy's relations with an uncertainly loyal, easily disaffected nobility. That is not the interest of the Auctrix at all, whose Nebuchadnezzar seems to be able to count on perfect submissiveness at home. So Nebuchadnezzar's conference in 2:2-3 is not intended as a test of loyalty. And if those of us who are disposed to ask such questions ask the question, Just why then does Nebuchadnezzar bother summoning his nobles?, the simple answer comes back, Because that is what Xerxes did, and Nebuchadnezzar is supposed to look, at least a little, like Xerxes.

Finally there is the problem of Bethulia. At Jdt 3:9-10 Holofernes reaches Esdraelon and encamps apparently not far to the west of Scythopolis. The reaction of Judea is given in the following chapter: it is assumed that Holofernes intends to make for Jerusalem and destroy the Temple, even as he has destroyed so many other shrines of subject peoples; the inhabitants of the northern hill country prepare apparently for siege; and Joakim the high priest instructs the inhabitants of Bethulia and Betomesthaim, the latter or both of which seem to be somewhere to the south or southwest of Esdraelon and to the north or northeast of Dothan, to take control of the ascents into the hill country, "because through them was the way leading to Judea, and it would be easy to check the advancing enemy, the path of advance being narrow, enough for a maximum of two men" (4:7). The issue will show that it is precisely by Bethulia that Holofernes wants to pass.

The problem of Bethulia is really twofold. First, if it is the prime intention of Holofernes at this point in his campaign to take Jerusalem--that is not made explicit, but the assumption of the Judeans at 4:1-3 is never doubted, and Judith later will impress Holofernes with her promise to lead him to Jerusalem, at 11:19--, then why does he not choose the much easier way to get there, from Scythopolis south along the west bank of the Jordan to the vicinity of Jericho, and only then westward into hill country, and a much shorter stretch of it too, until he reaches the capital? Not only does this impractical strategy strike us as being the most unlikely brainchild of any prudent commander; but also there seems to be no precedent for it either in the Bible or in the history of Israel. All invaders entering the Jordan valley from the north and heading for Jerusalem, from Sennacherib to the Seleucids, seem to have been able to get there without encountering major military obstacles. Or do we know of any of them being held up in the hills south of Esdraelon? In the second century B.C.E. it certainly was not true that Syrian invaders could find access to the Judean heartland only by way of the northern hill country, when Judas Maccabeus and his successors had to fight battles to the west and to the south of Jerusalem, and in its very vicinity.

The second part of the problem is: What specifically are the defensive tactics that the people of Bethulia are supposed to take up in order to control their narrow mountain pass? This is most unclear. We do not find a Hellenistic phalanx of hoplites blocking the pass, nor do hilltop guerrillas send missiles down upon the Assyrians as they attempt to defile. So are the Bethulians obeying the command of Joakim, or not? They are, but with gestures that must strike us as rather feckless: what seem to be some sort of earthworks they throw across the passes, they strew stumbling blocks in the plains, and they get ready to hunker down behind the new walls of their mountain fastnesses (5:1). It is little wonder that the job of laying siege to Bethulia should turn out to be so easy (7:1-18). What is more of a wonder is that Holofernes does not just turn his back on Bethulians, once he has chased them inside their walls, and head toward Jerusalem.

To make sense of this we need to remember a few of the things that the Auctrix is interested in. She is interested in locating her heroine at some distance from Jerusalem, independent of the Temple (cf. 9:1b--a rival cult?) and beyond the manipulation of the hierarchy, but at the same time responsible for the deliverance of Jerusalem; she is interested in presenting Judith as the only effectual defender of Bethulia; she is interested in the story of Dinah and Shechem, and in vindicating the vengeance of Simeon (9:2-4); she is interested, says Toni Craven, in mountains and hilltops.[5] And beyond all these interests of hers, she is absolutely required by the story she is telling to bring up the curtain on two scenes, the only two which are strictly necessary: the besieged town, being the home of the heroine; and the camp of the besiegers, in particular the tent of the villainous enemy general.

The location of Bethulia satisfies some of these interests: it is distant from Jerusalem; it is with but a slight strain in the neighborhood of Shechem; and it is in the hill country. But now the Auctrix faces the problem of having to keep Holofernes pinned at that location long enough for Judith to have time to get at him. There is no good strategic reason, as we have seen, for his hanging around there; the Bible is no help in offering any, nor is the history of Israel.

Her solution, of course, is to borrow Thermopylae from Herodotus (for the disposition of the pass, see vii.176; for the battle, vii.201-233). By suggesting that Holofernes' path to Jerusalem is like Xerxes' path to Athens and the other Greek cities by way of Thermopylae: that is, by suggesting that Holofernes wants to capture Jerusalem, that his only way of getting there is through the narrow passes in the hill country south of Esdraelon, and that it is very easy to block his progress through those passes, all of which the Auctrix accomplishes by 4:7: she is able to establish that Holofernes has no choice but to confront Bethulia, that he will not be able to leave that region until he has decisively defeated the Bethulians, and that Judith's offer to betray her countrymen and guide him through Judea to Jerusalem at 11:19 will appear to him very attractive.

Having established all that, she is in no way compelled to prove it, her style being what it is. The Thermopylae parallel is at once dropped. There are no Israelite hoplites at Bethulia; only one person in Bethulia is allowed to be heroic, and that is Judith. And since the story of Judith is necessarily the story of a siege, the Israelites of Bethulia shift their priorities from defending the mountain passes to defending the walls of their town, so smoothly that we hardly notice passing by the end of chap. 7 into a strange new narrative predicament.

Can we detect a Herodotean presence farther on in Judith? Probably not. But it is worth noting that the heroine has something in common not only with Ephialtes, the Greek traitor at Thermopylae, but also with the false traitor Themistocles, the Athenian leader who promises the Persians that he will surrender the Athenian fleet to them, and so lure their own ships into a risky position, resulting in their terrific defeat, at

Salamis. Moreover both Themistocles and Judith are first introduced in their respective stories as correct and encouraging interpreters of divine will to a dismayed group of their fellow citizens (for Themistocles and the oracle, see vii.143-144; for Salamis, viii.40-95). It is not impossible, then, that Themistocles may have served as a model for Judith. But that would be a rather more abstract kind of borrowing than how we saw the Auctrix used Book vii of Herodotus, and so probably requires a different argument in its defense. It is just as likely that we find in this a sign of a literary taste for the Greek historiographical style, especially the Herodotean style, serving as a model for prose fiction, a taste that would include the liar/hero, like Themistocles and like Judith, in its stock of admirable characters. On a different note, but which is no doubt a sign of the same thing, we recall that Herodotus locates a great deal of important history in bedrooms; and so there is no need to be surprised that Holofernes should meet with catastrophe in his bedroom.[6]

In conclusion it is hoped that this examination has made a Judith/Herodotus connection seem much more credible than it seemed in the past. The method it is based on has sought out problem spots in the first half of Judith that are more or less solved or explicated when they are considered to be adaptations of Herodotean material. But once the connection is established on the basis of these few spots, it is possible to re-read Judith with a new appreciation of how well the Auctrix understood Herodotus' narrative art, and how wisely she adapted it to her own ends. For example, the war between Nebuchadnezzar and Arphaxad in chap. 1 is a brilliant adaptation for her short story form of what Herodotus accomplishes in a much more leisurely way, the magnification of the eastern empire's might through a description of its earlier triumphs. And the character of Achior shows another aspect of the Auctrix' genius: learned in biblical literature and acquainted as well with Greek historiography, she is able to combine elements from both traditions into an interesting and effective new creation.

We may as well admit at once, that when we say the Auctrix was acquainted with Greek historiography, we may be talking only about Herodotus, but we may also mean something more. Once it is allowed that the Auctrix knew Herodotus, it must also be allowed that she is likely to have known other Greek authors as well. Is there evidence in Judith of any non-Herodotean Greek source? Probably there is, for those with eyes to see it. Moses Hadas, for one, detected the close resemblance between the story of the besieged Bethulians, lacking water, agreeing to surrender if no relief comes by the fifth day (7:30-31), and at last saved by divine intercession at the hand of Judith, and a story told in the Chronicle of Lindos about a siege of that city by the Persians, its lack of water, and its deliverance from having to surrender at the end of a five-day truce by a great rainfall sent by Zeus, with whom their patroness Athena had interceded; the goddess then unnerved the Persian commander by a personal epiphany. If that is another Greek story that the Auctrix liked and appropriated--and of course she would be interested in stories about sieges--, we must once again applaud her genius in adapting something so foreign to an impeccably Jewish setting.

And given her talent for compressing and adapting a story that interests her, is it impossible to discover beneath Jdt 1:13-15 a version of the final defeat and death of Darius III? Alexander defeated Darius in 330 B.C.E. at Gaugamela, near ancient Nineveh; Darius withdrew to Ecbatana, hoping to gather fresh support; Alexander took first Babylon, then Susa, then Persepolis, burning the palace there (cf. 1:14), then at last turned north against Ecbatana and Darius; Darius fled toward Ragae, then beyond it toward Hyrcania; Alexander pursued, and just as he reached Darius, the Persian king was fatally wounded by his own people (Arrian, An. iii.19-21). Aside from the necessary difference of names, only the last detail is remarkably different from the account in Judith of the death of Arphaxad. And that is just the sort of thing that the Auctrix would have altered: Nebuchadnezzar, himself plunging the fatal pikes into his foe, comes across as altogether more terrible than poor Alexander, gazing ruefully on the corpse of Darius.

Let us close with two questions touching on larger issues in Judith studies, which other students of Judith and of contemporary Jewish literature will be able to answer better than the present writer.

1. Can we be certain that the Septuagint text of Judith represents an original version of the story of Judith ancestral to all others? This student of Judith is doubtful. As was said above in another context, the story of Judith is the story of a siege; and so in principle we should grant priority to a tradition, perhaps found in one or more of the midrashim, that restricts itself to the context of a siege, presenting it with greatest simplicity and directness; other matters, like Jerusalem vs.

Bethulia as the original besieged site, for the moment can be left aside. As for the Septuagint Judith, it has been observed here that one of the principal narrative techniques of the Auctrix is to borrow narrative elements from other sources and adapt them to her own text, but in a way that allows a certain incoherence to remain; but this is especially true of the first half of the book, i.e. chaps. 1 to 7. It was also observed that the invasion story and the siege story do not stand in a quite logical relation to one another. It might be possible to conclude that the story of Judith that begins in chap. 8 is not original with the Auctrix; rather, that she only worked it up in accord with her own interests, fashioning for it a seven-chapter prologue.

2. Is it possible that in the second or first centuries B.C.E. an author writing in Hebrew and learned in biblical literature also knew Greek and was acquainted with any of the Greek classics? There seems to be a pattern of attributing a Greek literary education only to those Jewish writers who wrote Greek of a good quality, not to those who wrote it more colloquially or barbarically, and a fortiori not to those who wrote in a Semitic language. So what happens to the pattern if the Auctrix turns out to have known Herodotus? Would it be preferable to conclude that not only did the Auctrix know Greek, but the original language of Judith is Greek, only cleverly disguised to look like a translation from Hebrew? Or on the other hand would we like it more if the Auctrix were thought to be ignorant of Greek, and to have picked up these stories out of Herodotus, the Chronicle of Lindos, etc., from some purely oral story-telling source that passed along the gems of Greek historiography to barbarian nations? Can a place be found for a Jewish writer who could read Greek--and Ionic at that--and yet preferred to write in Hebrew?

---

[1]See Moses Hadas, Hellenistic Culture: Fusion and Diffusion (New York and London: W.W. Norton & Company, 1959) 165-169, and Arnaldo Momigliano, "Biblical Studies and Classical Studies: Simple Reflections about Historical Method," BA 45 (1982) 227-228, for favorable presentations of the idea. The relevant section of Momigliano's article is printed by Carey A. Moore, interested but not committed, in his commentary on Judith: Judith (AB 40; Garden City, NY: Doubleday, 1985) 154-155.

[2]This paper is a newer, neater version, I hope also an improved one, of a paper read at the 1988 Annual Meeting of the Society of Biblical Literature, in Chicago. I am grateful to all who offered comments and encouragement, and especially to William Adler, Shaye Cohen, Louis Feldman and Richard Pervo.

[3]The words translated by "there was talk...of punishing" are <u>egeneto logos...ekdikēsai</u>. This is not impeccable classical syntax; as a result, the notoriously slippery noun <u>logos</u>, the meaning of which a "good" author would have fixed by clearer syntax and context, is hard to interpret. "There was talk of punishing" might be supposed to mean more fully, "There was deliberation taken with a view to punishing," or even, "A speech was made, proposing the punishment of." Nor is that all. It is possible that <u>egeneto logos ekdikēsai</u> might be meant to translate a Hebrew original something like this: <u>wayhî dābār linqōm</u>. In late biblical texts, <u>dābār</u> followed by an infinitive can mean a decree or official command to do something (cf. 2 Chr 30:5; a less clear example is at Dan 9:25, where <u>dābār</u> is probably a prophetic word rather than a decree). So the difficult words in Jdt 2:1 could perhaps be translated, "There was issued a decree ordering the punishment of." That is indeed more vivid than the Greek; it sounds biblical enough, and accords with how <u>logos</u> is used elsewhere in Judith, for example at 2:3. But whether it gives a quite satisfactory sense is uncertain, seeing that it is not obvious how to relate a decree in 2:1 to the campaign conference of 2:2-3, or to the instructions to Holofernes, 2:4-13; to say nothing of the most basic question, To whom might such a decree be addressed?

[4]Another possible Herodotean model for this verse, one that would keep the palace discourse more appropriate to the monarch's fiery personality, is at v. 105: after the destructive Athenian adventure at Sardis, Darius is said not only to have prayed for divine assistance in punishing the Athenians, of whom he seems not to have heard before, but also to have ordered a slave to remind him of them daily just before dinner; we are told again about this slave at vi. 94.

[5]Toni Craven, <u>Artistry and Faith in the Book of Judith</u> (SBLDS 70; Chico: Scholars Press, 1983) 79-80.

[6]In her review of Richard I. Pervo's <u>Profit with Delight: The Literary Genre of the Acts of the Apostles</u>, in <u>JAAR</u> 58 (1990) 307-310, Marion L. Soards argues that a text like Acts can be more conveniently compared, with respect to genre, to ancient historiography than to the ancient novel, which is Pervo's direction; and that insofar as the narrative of Acts is entertaining, it functions precisely as an ancient history ought to function, Herodotus leading the way in this regard. That is a valuable and important observation. We may wish to follow it up by asking more generally why ancient historiography seems to have been so useful a discovery for the biblical tradition. This observer's guess is that the value of historiography for Jews and Christians, who applied it for the most part to one or another kind of hagiography, lay in its balance of a conservative, ancestor-regarding, community-regarding concern for truth--historiography claiming basically to tell the truth--, especially the truths traditionally valued by the community, against the more free and personal celebration of individual experience. One of the wonderful effects of Judith is to assure the Jewish reader of the value of her Jewish identity even while she is amazed, and amused, by the bizarre and inimitable sanctity of the heroine. That Judith was received as genuine history already in the time of Clement of Rome is testimony to its success in remaining faithful to the community and its truths.

WHY WASN'T THE BOOK OF JUDITH INCLUDED
IN THE HEBREW BIBLE?

Carey A. Moore
Gettysburg College

It is not surprising that for two thousand years Jews and, especially, Christians[1] have been mentioning Queen Esther and the widow Judith in the same breath. After all, both women are Jewish heroines in popular books named after them. Both women were very beautiful, resourceful, and brave. Finally, the books bearing their names are among the most interesting and skillfully written of the Bible.

Nonetheless, these two books experienced drastically different fates. Today, Esther is sacred scripture for both Jews and Christians while Judith is regarded as noncanonical, or apocryphal, by Jews and Protestants but as deutero- [i.e., second] canonical by Roman Catholics.[2]

That Jews accepted Esther but rejected Judith becomes very puzzling when one realizes that Judith is obviously a religious book while Esther, at least on its surface, is not,[3] neither God nor such distinctive Jewish themes and institutions as the Law, covenant, prayer, sacrifice, the Temple, or kashrût[4] being so much as mentioned in it. By contrast, these and many other religious beliefs and practices characteristic of biblical Judaism are inextricably woven into Judith - and in quite orthodox fashion. Why, then, was the "orthodox" book of Judith not included in the Jewish canon?

I. The So-Called "Council" of Jamnia[5]

Certainly, the old scholarly answer (i.e., that in ca. 90 CE the Jewish Council of Jamnia closed the Hebrew canon, firmly and finally, rejecting in the process what is known as the Old Testament apocrypha,[6] including Judith) will not do. I use the word "old" because the Jamnia theory, which was first broached in 1871 by H. Graetz who posited the Council of Jamnia as leading to the closing of the canon to 189 CE, received its first popular presentations by F. Buhl in 1892 and by H.E. Ryle in 1904.[7] As the theory generally stands, shortly after the destruction of the Jewish temple and nation, the rabbinic "synod" or "council" at Jamnia, somewhere around 90 CE, finalized the canonization of the Hebrew Bible, closing the Jewish canon for all time. Moreover, it was believed by scholars that the rabbis had resolved to exclude from their canon Jewish/Christian apocalyptic and apocryphal works appearing in the Septuagint,[8] especially those books composed originally in Greek.[9]

Up through the first-half of the twentieth century, the theory that the "Council of Jamnia" closed the Hebrew canon and, in effect, rejected the apocrypha was the prevailing scholarly view,[10] and it still has its adherents today.[11]

But starting in the early 1950's, some scholars, such as H. H. Rowley,[12] began to have reservations about the role of Jamnia, especially as to whether it actually had the binding authority that the word "council" or "synod" has had in Christian church history:

> It is, indeed, doubtful how far it is correct to speak of the Council Jamnia...discussions . . . took place there . . . but we know of no formal or binding decisions that were made, and it is probable that the discussions were informal, though none the less helping to crystallize and to fix more firmly the Jewish tradition [italics added].[13]

Today, thanks primarily to the works of D. N. Freedman, J. P. Lewis and S. Z. Leiman,[14] scholars like B. S. Childs, R. Beckwith, and S. J. D. Cohen are putting far less emphasis on Jamnia's central role, arguing that there is a lack of evidence for most of it.[15] The so-called "council" or "synod" of Jamnia (beginning perhaps as early as 75 CE or as late as 117 CE)[16] is better understood as an academy, school, assembly, or, even, a court.[17]

The canonization of the Hebrew Bible, scholars now say, was not an event, done once-and-for-all by an elite group of rabbis. Rather, it was an extended, three-stage,[18] dynamic process[19] engaged in by the Jewish community, whereby, first, the Law (Hebrew twrh) or Pentateuch, then the Prophets (nby'ym),[20] and, lastly, the Writings (ktwbym), or Hagiographa,[21] were canonized.

Although the approximate dates for the canonization of the Law[22] and of the Prophets[23] is still debated by scholars, it is relevant for our purposes to note that recent studies suggest that the Hagiographa was canonized in either the first[24] or even the second[25] century BCE (!). In other words, most, if not all, of the Hebrew Bible had, in effect, already been canonized prior to the Jamnia Council, although the canonicity of several biblical books (notably, Esther, Qoheleth, and the Song of Songs) was still being disputed by some Jews into the third or fourth century CE.

As for the old Alexandrian Canon hypothesis[26] (i.e., that the apocrypha of the Greek Old Testament had originally been approved by the supposed "Sanhedrin in Alexandria" and that the Jamnian rabbis had rejected the apocryphal books because of their having been originally composed in Greek or in Egypt[27]), Hebrew and/or Aramaic copies of some of those very books have been found among the Dead Sea Scrolls (e.g., Tobit,[28] Jubilees,[29] and Enoch[30])!

Although, to date, no copy of Judith in Hebrew or Aramaic[31] has been found at Qumran, the internal evidence for a Hebrew <u>Vorlage</u> for its Greek version is quite strong, if not conclusive.[32]

In any event, the judicious conclusion of Lewis[33] some twenty-five years ago regarding the Jamnia Council is worth repeating:

> Of the apocryphal books, only Ben Sira is mentioned by name in rabbinic sources. This would be true of both pre- and post-Jabneh sources...Though it is often assumed that the apocrypha were excluded at that time [i.e., at Jamnia ca. 90 CE], <u>no text specifically attributes a discussion of the apocryphal books to Jabneh</u>. That the apocrypha were discussed by the gathering is a conjecture incapable of proof. For that matter, no book is mentioned in the sources as being excluded from the canon at Jabneh.[34]

Thus, the old, easy argument that the Council of Jamnia, somewhere around 90 CE, omitted Judith from the Hebrew canon because it was composed in Greek is no longer persuasive.

II. The Composition Date of Judith

If the third section of the Hebrew canon was closed as early as the first or even the second century BCE, then Judith's date of composition may be the principal reason for its not being included in the Hagiographa. Despite the tale's explicit late Persian setting,[35] the book was redacted in the Hasmonean Period, as its striking parallels with the days of Judas Maccabeus clearly indicate.[36]

Recently, Cohen has dated Judith's redaction to the second century BCE.[37] Putting a new twist on Zeitlin's old argument that Jamnia rejected Judith for <u>halakhic</u> reasons (i.e., although Achior the Ammonite believed in God and was converted to Judaism by being circumcised [Jdt 14:10], Achior was not baptized/immersed in water nor did he offer a sacrifice in the Temple, all of which were rabbinic requirements by the second century CE),[38] Cohen rightly points out, however, that we do not really know what all the first and second century BCE requirements for conversion were; for there are no second temple texts attesting to immersion and sacrifice as required rituals of conversion.

To be sure, both Qumran and Christianity had their baptisms, but this does not necessarily mean that both rituals were required by Jews a century or so earlier. According to Cohen, then, Achior's being circumcised is not only fully in keeping with the ritual practice during the crisis in the early days of the Maccabean Revolt but no mention of either Achior's baptism or sacrifice may be an argument (albeit from silence) for Judith's being dated to the second century BCE!

Beckwith sees in Judith's immersing herself rather than just washing her hands before prayer (cf. Jdt 12:5-9) evidence of the book's being written or redacted in the second century BCE.[39] For by the latter half of the second century BCE, the Pharisees had substituted the washing of one's hands, Beckwith maintains, for immersion (cf. Ep. Arist. 305).

One might counter that here, as T. Craven's superb rhetorical analysis of the book of Judith has shown often elsewhere,[40] literary rather than ritualistic considerations may have been foremost, that is, for Judith and her maid to make good their escape, they had to establish a pattern of going outside the camp to bathe (cf. Jdt 12:5-9; 13:9-10). Beckwith also argues that the book of Judith is more of Pharisaic than Essene origin because festival observance of Fridays (cf. Jdt 8:6) was part of Pharisaic tradition (cf. m. Ta'an. 4.2; m. Ḥag. 3.7).[41]

If one does accept a second century BCE date for the composition of Judith, then it might be argued that just as the book of Daniel (generally dated to ca. 164 BCE) was accepted into the Palestinian canon, so Judith may also have been accepted and then, for whatever reason/s,[42] subsequently excluded. Certainly there is no reason, in principle at least, why this could not have happened among one or more Jewish groups,[43] although, it must be emphasized, there is no evidence of such a debate about Judith in any rabbinic literature of the first or second century BCE or CE.

I would further counter that while Jewish communities in Palestine could easily maintain that Daniel had been actually composed during the late exilic or early post-exilic period, no such argument could be made for Judith, its Persian setting notwithstanding, because of the story's striking similarities to, if not certain dependence upon, Judas Maccabeus's victorious struggle over General Nicanor (ca. 161 BCE).

Cohen and Beckwith may very well be correct that Judith was composed or at least redacted in the second century BCE; but as I have argued elsewhere,[44] a more likely date is some time during the reign of either John Hyrcanus I (135-104 BCE), possibly after his annexation and "integration" of Samaritan territory in 107 BCE or, less likely, of Alexander Janneus (103-76 BCE). If a Hasmonean date is correct, then Judith was composed too late to have been included in the Writings.

III. Some Other Considerations

But even if Judith was composed early enough to have been included in the Writings, it was not. Although space here does not permit my presenting, in detail, other possible reasons for its not being part of the Hagiographa, I have done so in a recent article elsewhere,[45] showing that early critics of the book could have found any number of objections, or "flaws," to it (although the book's critics have often said as much about themselves and their times as they have about the tale itself).[46]

Briefly, there is the book's questionable historicity or veracity, especially with regard to those historical and geographical anachronisms, inconsistencies, and errors abounding in its first three chapters.[47] Or, the tale's "pro-feminist stance" may have been simply too radical for the males who determined the Hebrew canon.[48] Then too, many people - past and present, Jewish and Christian - have viewed Judith herself as deficient in character[49] and immoral in her conduct.[50] In any event, Judith was, ironically, the saint[51] who murdered for her people.

Failure to recognize irony as the quintessential characteristic of the book is the primary reason for so many of the misinterpretations of it and may just be the clue to many of its historical, geographical, and moral problems[52] as well as the reason why it, in contrast to the "secular" book of Esther, did not enter the Hebrew canon. Judith herself is most ironic. Although shapely, beautiful, and wealthy, she lived an abstemious and celibate existence, one filled with prayer and self-denial. Childless, she gave new life to her people. She not only prayed for a deceitful tongue,[53] but actually begged Israel's merciful God for strength to cut off a defenseless man's head. The ultimate irony, of course, is that a deeply religious woman became revered, not for her piety but her murderous act. Such ironies can fascinate one reader and repel another.

Why was Judith not included in the Hebrew canon while the "godless" book of Esther was? Many plausible reasons can be offered, but the simple fact is that we do not know. While scholars naturally look for the reason, maybe there is not just one. Rather, just as in secular elections in which the individual voters cast their ballots for or against a particular candidate for one or more reasons, be those reasons valid or not, so the "voting" of the Hebrew people for or against a particular book's inclusion in the Jewish canon may have been the result of a number of considerations. It was, ultimately, the Jewish community, sometimes over a long period of time, that determined which Jewish books "defiled the hands." For better or worse, the book of Judith was not included among them.

Finally, the story of Judith has as its basic ingredients four motifs about which people, ancient and modern, can feel very strongly and differently: God, power, sex, and death. Moreover, the tale embodies two of the most popular but controversial aphorisms of many who, in any day, call themselves Jews or Christians:

All's fair in love and war.

The end justifies the means.

Small wonder this little book has been so popular - and so controversial!

[1] Among the Church Fathers, the three earliest allusions to the book of Judith are intimately tied up with the story of Esther, namely, in 1 Clement 55, dating from the first century CE; Stromata 4.19 of Clement of Alexandria (150?-?215); and the Constitutions of the Holy Apostles 5.3.20 (ca. 380). In all three, the bravery of Judith and Esther is noted. Moreover, the books of Esther and Judith are mentioned side by side (regardless of whether they were regarded as canonical) in the biblical list of Athanasius of Alexandria (293?-373), Augustine (354-430), Innocent I (reigned 401-417), Pseudo-Gelasius, Cassiodorus (485?-?585), Anonymi Dial. Timothei et Aquilae, Junilius (fl. ca 542), Isidorus of Miletus (560-636), Liber sacramentorum, Nicephorus of Constantinople (758?-829), and Ebedjesu, as well as the Council of Carthage (397) and LXX[B].

[2] Protestants include in their Old Testament only those books found in the Hebrew Bible. For Roman Catholics, Judith's canonical status, like that of other deuterocanonical books, was re-affirmed by the Council of Trent in 1546. For details on Judith's earlier canonical status among various eastern and western Church Fathers, see

my Judith, AB 40; Garden City, NY: Doubleday, 1985) 90-91.

[3]For a discussion of this and related problems in the book of Esther, see my "Eight Questions Most Frequently Asked About the Book of Esther," BR 3 (1987) 16-31.

[4]Fasting is the only distinctively religious practice mentioned in Esther (cf. 4:16; 9:31).

[5]Jamnia (Hebr. Yavneh), nine miles N-NE of Ashdod and four miles inland from the Mediterranean Sea, is where the rabbis first assembled after the destruction of Jerusalem in 70 CE.

[6]S. Zeitlin says, "There must have been opposition to other books of which we have no historical records. On the other hand there must have been many in favor of the inclusion of a number of the books in the canon which are now commonly called apocrypha, particularly those books which bore such titles as Enoch, Ezra, Wisdom of Solomon, Baruch, etc." ("Jewish Apocryphal Literature," JQR 11 [1950] 23). Cf. also B. Metzger, An Introduction to the Apocrypha (New York: Oxford University Press, 1957) 8; see also C. T. Fritsch, "Apocrypha," IDB 1:163.

[7]H. Graetz, Kohelet oder der salomonische Prediger (Leipzig: Winter, 1871) 165-66; see also his "Der Abschluss des Kanons des Alten Testaments," MGWJ 35 (1886) 281-298; F. Buhl, Canon and Text of the Old Testament (Edinburgh: T.& T. Clark, 1892) 24; H.E. Ryle, The Canon of the Old Testament (London: MacMillan, 1904) 182-83.

[8]It was through this pre-Christian Greek version of the Jewish scriptures, which later also contained other Jewish/Christian religious books, that the Christian Church came to know the Jewish scriptures.

[9]First proposed in modern times by J.S. Semler, Abhandlung von freier Untersuchung des Canons I (Halle: C.H. Hemmerde, 1771). Scholars who subscribed to the "Alexandrian Canon hypothesis" (see n. 26) could call attention to the fact that for a Jewish scroll to be canonical (lit. "to make the hands unclean") it had to be not only divinely inspired (lit. "be spoken by the Holy Spirit" [t. Yad. 2.14; b. Meg. 7a]), but also be written on parchment, in ink, in the original Hebrew or Aramaic language, and in the square script (m. Yad. 4:5).

[10]Scholars subscribing to this theory included W.O.E. Oesterley, The Books of the Apocrypha (London: SPCK, 1915) 173; M.L. Margolis, The Hebrew Scriptures in the Making (Philadelphia: Jewish Publication Society of America, 1922) 84-89; R.H. Pfeiffer, Jr., Introduction to the Old Testament (New York: Harper, 1941) 64; R. Meyer, "The Canon and the Apocrypha in Judaism," TDNT 3. 978-987; A.C. Sundberg, Jr., The Old Testament of the Early Church (HTS 20; Cambridge: Harvard University, 1964) 113, 127; and O. Eissfeldt, The Old Testament: An Introduction (New York: Harper & Row, 1965) 568.

[11]M. Avi-Yonah, "Yavneh," Encyclopaedia Judaica (Jerusalem: Keter, 1971) 9.1177; E. Robertson, "Jamnia," Encyclopaedia Britannica 1970, 12.871; and G.W. Anderson, "Canonical and Non-Canonical," in The Cambridge History of the Bible (ed. P.R. Ackroyd; Cambridge: Cambridge University Press, 1970) 1.133; and J.A. Sanders, Torah and Canon (Philadelphia: Fortress, 1972) 94-95, although in his Canon and Community: A Guide to Canonical Criticism (Philadelphia: Fortress, 1984; 9-12, 35) Sanders takes a

more cautious and qualified view.

[12]The Growth of the Old Testament (London: Hutchison University Library, 1950) 170. See also G.W. Anderson, A Critical Introduction to the Old Testament (London: Duckworth, 1959) 12-13.

[13]Ibid., 12-13. Sundberg (The Old Testament of the Early Church 127) seems to suggest something similar.

[14]D.N. Freedman, "Canon of the O.T.," IDBSuppl, 134-36. Freedman's words in private correspondence with me are very apropos: "What do we really know about the Council of Jamnia? Everybody quotes everybody else about this famous or infamous Council, but what are the ancient sources, and what are reasonable inferences about its activity? Personally, I think it was a non-event, and not much happened, unlike the Council of Nicaea for example. It would be refreshing if someone cited actually ancient sources for this Council and its work." J.P. Lewis, "What Do We Mean by Jabneh?" JBR 32 (1964) 125-32. This issue and related ones are also treated by Lewis in his soon-to-be published "Jamnia After Twenty-Five Years," presented at the 1988 Annual Meeting of the Society of Biblical Literature in Chicago. S.Z. Leiman, The Canonization of Hebrew Scripture: The Talmudic and Midrashic Evidence (Hamden, CT: Archon Books, 1976).

[15]Childs, Introduction to the Old Testament as Scripture (Philadelphia: Fortress, 1979) 53, 66. R. Beckwith, The Old Testament Canon of the New Testament Church and its Background in Early Judaism (Grand Rapids: Eerdmans, 1985) 276-77. S.J.D. Cohen, From the Maccabees to the Mishnah (Philadelphia: Westminster 1987) 174-95, 226-31.

[16]Leiman, The Canonization of Hebrew Scripture, 120-24.

[17]Lewis, "What Do We Mean by Yabneh?" 127-28.

[18]The earliest attestation to the existence of the three sections of the Hebrew canon, however, is the prologue to Ecclesiasticus, which may be dated to ca. 132 BCE.

[19]Childs rightly observes that "One cannot assume that one canonical section was tightly closed [italics added] before another was formed because of the lack of solid evidence from which to draw such a conclusion" (Introduction to the Old Testament as Scripture, 53).

[20]I.e., the Former Prophets (Joshua, Judges, Samuel, Kings) and the Latter Prophets (Isaiah, Jeremiah, Ezekiel, and the twelve minor prophets).

[21]According to an ancient Jewish tradition (Bar. b. Bat. 14b of the Talmud), the order is Ruth, Psalms, Job, Proverbs, Ecclesiastes, Song of Solomon, Lamentations, Daniel, Esther, Ezra-Nehemiah, and 1-2 Chronicles. This source, however, is not as ancient as the "list" of, say, Josephus (cf. Ag. Ap. 1.7 or 1.37-43 [see Beckwith, The Old Testament Canon, 206-07]) who gives a slightly different order. But in the ancient Hebrew and Greek lists there was some fluidity in the book listings of the Writings as well as the Prophets (ibid., 181-234).

[22]Canonization dates for the Law and for the Prophets vary greatly among scholars. For example, whereas Leiman (The Canonization of Hebrew Scripture, 20-24) concludes that

pre-Josianic written and canonical law corpora existed prior to ca. 621 BCE, and Freedman ("Canon of the O.T.", 99. 131-32) would date the Law and the Former Prophets, in some form, to ca. 550 BCE, most scholars date the canonization of the Law to about a century later; and the Prophets, still later.

[23]Although T.N. Swanson argues for the Prophets' canon being open well into the Christian era (The Closing of the Collection of Holy Scriptures: A Study in the History of the Canonization of the Old Testament [diss. Vanderbilt University, 1970]), Sir 46:1-49:13, dating to the early second century BCE, knows all the prophetic books in their canonical order.

[24]"Jewish sources such as the Apocrypha, Philo, and Josephus, as well as Christian sources reflecting Jewish practice, such as the New Testament and the church fathers, support the notion of a closed biblical canon in most Jewish circles through the first centuries before and after the Christian era...Critical analysis of the book of Daniel, evidence from the Apocrypha, and the newly discovered biblical texts in Hebrew and Greek (from Qumran, Nahal Hever, and elsewhere) suggest the possibility and likelihood that the biblical canon was closed in the Maccabean period. The talmudic and midrashic evidence is entirely consistent with a second century dating for the closing of the biblical canon." (Leiman, The Canonization of Hebrew Scripture 135)

[25]Cf. Beckwith (The Old Testament Canon, 152, 164-66), who dates the separation of the division of the Prophets and the Writings from the Law to 164 BCE, when Judas Maccabeus "gathered together for us all those writings" (2 Macc 2:14-15).

[26]For a detailed description as well as a refutation of it, see Sundberg, The Old Testament of the Early Church, 51-79.

[27]So J.E. Grabe, The History of the Seventy-Two Interpreters (London: J. Whitaker, 1715); and W.R. Churton, The Uncanonical and Apocryphal Scriptures (London, 1884).

[28]One Hebrew and four Aramaic copies of it have been identified (J.T. Milik, "La Patrie de Tobie," RB 73 [1966] 522-30).

[29]For details, see J.C. VanderKam, Textual and Historical Studies in the Book of Jubilees (HSM 14; Missoula: Scholars Press, 1977); E. Schurer, The History of the Jewish People in the Age of Jesus Christ (175 B.C.-A.D. 135) (3 vols.; rev. by G. Vermes, et al.; Edinburgh, T. & T. Clark, 1973-87) 3.1.

[30]There are eleven Aramaic copies; see J.T. Milik and M. Black, The Books of Enoch: Aramaic Fragments of Qumrân Cave 4 (Oxford: Oxford University Press, 1976).

[31]E.J. Bruns insisted on an Elephantine and Aramaic Vorlage for Judith ("Judith or Jael?" CBQ 16 [1954] 12-14; cf. also his "The Genealogy of Judith," CBQ 18 [1956] 19-22); but, unfortunately, he offered no philological or linguistic evidence for this view.

[32]G.W.E. Nickelsburg evidently subscribes to a Hebrew archetype (Jewish Literature Between the Bible and the Mishnah [Philadelphia: Fortress, 1981] 109); but T. Craven believes "the Greek text could have been written from the outset in elegant hebraicised Greek" (Artistry and Faith in the Book of Judith [SBLDS 70; Chico: Scholars Press, 1983] 5). For examples of Hebraisms in Judith, see F. Zimmerman, "Aids for the

Recovery of the Hebrew Original of Judith," JBL 57 (1938) 67-74; see also my Judith, 66-67.

[33]"What Do We Mean by Jabneh?" 131.

[34]Lewis ("What Do We Mean by Jabneh?" 131). He also rightly concluded that t. Yad. 2:13 ("The Gilyonim and the books of the Minim [heretics] do not defile the hands. The books of Ben Sira and all the books which were written since that time do not defile the hands" [cf. also y. Sanh. 10:1, 28]), the principal text invoked for arguing that Jamnia excluded the apocrypha, is a passage without date or occasion. The Gilyonim, Lewis maintains, refers to the Gospels, not the apocrypha (ibid., 132).

[35]For example, major and minor characters have names common in the Persian period, and there are allusions to certain Persian campaigns, accomplishments, practices and terms. For details on these and other types of examples, see Pfeiffer, History of New Testament Times, 293-95; also my Judith, 49-50, 55.

[36]As Nickelsburg has rightly noted, "The story of Judith has striking similarities to the time of Judas Maccabeus. Nebuchadnezzar may be understood as a figure for Antiochus IV... The defeat of a vastly superior invading army parallels Judas's defeat of the Syrians. Especially noteworthy are the similarities between this story and Judas's defeat of Nicanor...Nicanor's subsequent threat against the Temple, his defeat and decapitation, and the public display of his head in Jerusalem all find remarkable counterparts in the story of Judith (cf. 1 Macc 7:33-50)" (Jewish Literature Between The Bible and the Mishnah 108-09).

[37]From the Maccabees to the Mishnah, 50-55.

[38]"Proselytes and Proselytism During the Second Commonwealth in the Early Tannaitic Period," in Harry Austryn Wolfson Jubilee Volume (Jerusalem: American Academy for Jewish Research, 1965). H.M. Orlinsky also regards Achior's not being baptized as the halakhic reason for the rabbis' rejecting the book (Essays in Biblical and Bible Translation [New York: KTAV, 1974] 279-81).

[39]The Old Testament Canon, 17.

[40]See Craven, Artistry and Faith, passim.

[41]Thus far, no Semitic or Greek text of Judith has been found at Qumran.

[42]For example, given the hostility existing between Jews and Samaritans - so clearly expressed in, say, the Gospels of the New Testament - later Jews may have disapproved of the book's accepting attitude toward the towns of Samaria, in general (Jdt 4:4, 6; 15:4), and, especially, of making a Samaritan woman and her kinsmen the "saviors" of Jerusalem and its Temple.

[43]In fact, S.M. Zarb argues precisely that for Judith as well as for Tobit and Maccabees (De Historia Canonis Utriusque Testamenti [Rome: Pont. Institutum 'Angelicum', 1934] 58-63), but Beckwith characterizes the attempt as "without the slightest success" (The Old Testament Canon, 376). It should be remembered that according to Origen, (Letter to Africanus 13), the Jews did not include Judith or Tobit even among the "apocrypha,"

i.e., books stored away.

[44]*Judith*, 67-70.

[45]"The Case of the Pious Killer," Bible Review 6 (1990) 26-36. A number of the issues mentioned below have also been discussed in my *Judith* (passim).

[46]For details, see my *Judith*, 64-66.

[47]Ibid., 121-145.

[48]So Craven, Artistry and Faith, 117-18.

[49]Judith's conversations with Holofernes prove she was a shameless flatterer (Jdt 11:7-8), an equivocator (12:14, 18), and a bold-faced liar (11:10, 12-14, 18-19). Her double entendres and her ironic and ambiguous statements in her conversations with Holofernes are not her pious efforts to avoid lying but an expression of her (or, better, the author's) sense of humor.

[50]Judith was a ruthless assassin (Jdt 13:7-8), with no respect for the dead (13:9-10, 15).

[51]By the standards of her day, Judith lived a saintly life (Jdt 8:4-6, 8; 12:4; 16:22-24).

[52]See my *Judith*, 78-85.

[53]Prior to Judith's leaving for the enemy camp, she prayed, "Grant me a beguiling tongue for wounding and bruising those who have terrible designs against your covenant and your sacred house, even against Mount Zion and the house your children possess" (Jdt 9:13).

JUDITH AND HOLOFERNES:
SOME OBSERVATIONS ON THE DEVELOPMENT
OF THE SCENE IN ART

Nira Stone

Jerusalem

In order to present the scene of Judith and Holofernes in art in the context of a seminar on the Book of Judith, I debated where to start and how to continue, and I could have chosen any number of approaches. For the sake of clarity, however, I decided to take a strictly diachronic approach. The dominant way Judith is presented is found from the fifteenth century on -- but was this true in earlier ages?

We shall examine, first of all, how Judith appears in art prior to the Renaissance.[1] I shall not present detailed stylistic or iconographic analyses of the various representations of Judith, but shall try to review the development of the Judith figure and the scenes associated with her action in Christian and Jewish art.

Like almost any subject today, that of Judith also has feminist implications, and although they will not be at the forefront of our presentation here, they cannot be ignored. After all, from very early times a female figure is presented as subduing her enemy by decapitation. This should not be viewed as excessive cruelty, but as an efficient, technical means of overcoming an enemy who is physically stronger and, sometimes, a warrior surrounded by guards. Artists were conscious of this in antiquity, as is exemplified in figures like the exultant Menead from the first century CE holding the head of her enemy in her left hand and waving her sword in her right.[2] Another interesting fact is that almost all the artists creating Judith up to modern times were men. So when we discuss the ways in which Judith was presented, we should bear that in mind. This is true especially when the feminine emotional approach is taken as seen through the eyes of the male artists.

The figure of Judith attracted artists of all generations, not just in the plastic arts. Music and literature, too, are full of Judith. She appears in Jewish Piyyutim of the twelfth century and in the Latin church hymns from the sixteenth century to the present. Operas and particularly operettas have been written, most recently by the Israeli composer Mordechai Seter in 1963. Literature, too, abounds with Judith. From the thirteenth century, for example, we have both an English epic and a High German poem entitled "Judith."[3]

73

In art Judith was constantly presented differently from other heroines of the Bible or the apocryphal literature. The reason was always the following. Although she resembles Jael and Esther more than Deborah, for she did not lead the people, but carried out an act of self-sacrifice and personal courage, still, nothing was demanded of her. She volunteered, initiated the plan, summoned the leaders of the people who came obediently, and she encouraged them. She remained celibate, pure in body as in soul also after the drama was over. These reasons combined to present her as a perfect heroine.

The chief ways she was presented in art are:

1. A Christian religious presentation which commenced in the early Middle Ages.

2. A national-patriotic way -- in Italian art of the Renaissance period.

3. A national-religious way -- in Jewish art from the Renaissance on.

4. The feminine-emotional way -- in modern art.

The two central points that attracted artists were her self-sacrifice in going to Holofernes' camp and the courage of the decapitation, and these two themes are dominant in the artistic representation.

Christian artists were the first to present the story of Judith in manuscripts from the ninth century, doubtless based upon earlier representations which have been lost. Prior to the ninth century we have only fragments of a fresco in the Church of S. Maria Antiqua in Rome. Medieval Christian artists, like the medieval writers, viewed Judith in terms of Christian symbolism: she represented the fighting Church, Christ's bride, in the fight against Satan, and also the Virgin crushing the head of the serpent.

The artistic descriptions may be divided into four chief types and we shall examine each of these:

A. The narrative descriptions of the whole story from beginning to end given on a single page or part of a page.

B. Epitomized representations of the moment of the decapitation alone, with or without a servant.

C. The expanded version.

D. Symbolic appearance of the figure of the heroine Judith in painting or sculpture, holding the sword of victory in her hand.

A. The Narrative Descriptions

1. After the appearance of the badly preserved scene in the Church of S. Maria Antiqua in Rome in the eighth century, the earliest example is a ninth-century Latin manuscript, the Carolingian Bible (figure 4).[4] Here the story is presented in three registers. The upper presents Judith's leaving Bethulia and her return there. At the left is the city surrounded by a wall in which the inhabitants accompany Judith and her servant on their way. On the right are the women returning, which concludes all that is related in the lower register. This phenomenon is one of contracted scenes.

The middle register shows on the right Judith and her servant sitting and waiting for the messenger who has just arrived and who brings her, on the left, to Holofernes who is seated upon a royal throne and looks rather like a Carolingian king, not an Assyrian or Persian one!

The lowest register describes, on the left, the moment of the decapitation. Holofernes is inside his gabled Carolingian palace, lying headless on the bed. To his left Judith is seated, still wielding her sword. The servant is seen gathering up the head. On the right, the women return to Bethulia, Judith proudly, with her head high, while the servant, with Holofernes' head in her hand, looks wonderingly at the arena of the terrible deed. As I have already observed, this return to Bethulia is taken up in the first register and closes a narrative cycle--what is called "a circular story."

In spite of the fact that this is the first known description in a Bible manuscript, it is doubtlessly based upon an earlier representation in which Judith returns to the city, the gates of which are locked and not, as in the picture before us, in which the scenes were contracted so as to save space. The dramatic emphasis here is upon the victorious return of Judith to Bethulia.

2. Since the development we are tracing cuts across borders and styles our example from the tenth century is in a Byzantine manuscript. The differences between this and the Carolingian Bible are minor: a slightly different stance of the figures and a slightly variant style. The conceptual development is common at this time to Western and to Byzantine art, and both are probably based on the same model.

3. The next example is the Greek tenth-century Leo Bible.[5] This is one of two isolated Byzantine examples in which Judith approaches her enemy from behind, unperceived. It is a good example of a misunderstood copy

of an earlier model. The inhabitants of Bethulia look out, yet Judith is not on the right, where she should be, but below. There she is led by the messenger to Holofernes who is missing from the picture. Judith at once sets about beheading Holofernes who is lying in an odd position and is presented as a young, shaven Greek king. Judith's return is missing here and below we find a scene entitled by its rubric "The Army of the Children of Israel conquering the Assyrians."

It is interesting to observe how the figures are represented in the terms of the artist's period. While in the previous example, a Latin manuscript of the Carolingian period, Holofernes was a Carolingian king, here he is a young Greek king, as seemed fitting to the Byzantine painter. 4. In the eleventh century Spanish Roda Bible, the first register is a schematic painting of the city, while on the left the citizens accompany the women who are setting forth.[6] The remaining registers may be described as follows:

The second register, on the left: Judith holding a Carolingian staff sets forth accompanied by her servant; on the right: The conclusion of the narrative, in the fashion of the "circular story." In the third register: The women before Holofernes who is seated on a royal throne, while in the background is the messenger who is presenting the women to him. In the fourth register, lower right: the moment after the decapitation -- Judith is putting the head into a basket, a sword is in her hand, on the bed is the headless body. Finally, in register two: Judith's return to Bethulia with the head. Once again, the scenes are held together as a circular story. 5. Sometimes we find unusual representations in certain manuscripts. One of them is the Arsenal Bible (figure 2).[7] This is a French Crusader Bible of the thirteenth century from Acre. Here the story covers two pages, each of which has three registers divided into smaller scenes.

On the first page, from left to right the scenes are:
1. The Assyrians threatening Bethulia.
2. The elders of the city in consultation.
3. The elders summoned to Judith's house.
4. Judith in Holofernes' tent.
5. The decapitation.
6. Judith returning victorious with Holofernes' head.
The unusual scenes are numbers 3 and 6.

Scene 3 is of great interest. It is divided into two parts. In the first part, at left two of the elders appear, summoned to Judith's house. Judith is seated at the right in widow's weeds. In the second part, on the right, Judith appears again, in glorious clothing before setting out for the Assyrian camp. This point is stressed in the book (10:1-5) but rarely appears in art. The transformation of Judith from a woman to an emissary of the people became a symbol of the ability of a widow, a person of inferior social status, to become a heroine and holder of high office.[8]

Another unusual scene on the same page is that of Judith's victory, on the lower right (scene 6). Here she stands on a platform, while the elders of Bethulia kneel before her. She is in the stance of an orans, with the head in her left hand. Naturally, the immediate association is of the Virgin standing in just this stance below the scene of Christ's Assumption to heaven. Judith is presented as a prefiguration of the Virgin and a symbol of the Church, at whose feet all the people are gathered.

6. The next example is from twelfth-century Germany (figure 3). This is "The Garden of Delights" or Hortus Deliciarum.[9] The manuscript is called "The Feminist" by scholars. In contrast to the preceding, which were all Bibles, this manuscript has two new qualities. First, it is an anthology of selected passages from the Bible, the Church Fathers, and from secular philosophers. The second new quality is the fact that it was composed by a very learned woman, herself the student of yet another prominent woman. The author was Herrad of Landsberg who served as the Abbess of the Convent of St. Ottile in Hohenberg in 1167 and whose teacher was the renowned scholar Abbess Relindis. Herrad devoted a good deal of her book to that special woman, Judith. It is not certainly known but it is presumed that she was also the artist who illustrated the manuscript.

Here the artist chose two scenes from the life of Judith which were set on a separate leaf, in two registers. The presentation is narrative, but it is very concentrated and might even be characterized as "Narrative-Symbolic." The first register is the moment of decapitation, together with the servant, inside the tent. The second is the return to Bethulia. The gates of the city are closed and two citizens are peeking out. At the right the head is already impaled on the wall in order to frighten the enemy.

7. A similar division into two also occurs in a Jewish manuscript of the fifteenth century from Germany.[10] This is a manuscript of a Book of Prayers and Varia (Mainz ?), dating from 1434 CE. The description of the

story of Judith is divided into two separate pictures on one page, in the part of the manuscript containing the Piyyutim for Hanukkah, including a narrative of Judith's deeds. We shall soon discuss the relationship between Judith and Hanukkah, in more detail.

In the upper picture, the scene is set in the camp of tents. Holofernes is lying on his bed and Judith is beheading him while soldiers sleep on the ground. In the lower picture, Judith returns with her servant to Bethulia, holding the severed head. On one of the towers a head, like that of Holofernes, can be seen. As in the Hortus Deliciarum, so here the artist stresses the characters' position inside or near the tent. This specific point recurs elsewhere, including another Jewish manuscript which relates Judith to Hanukkah and the Maccabees, a 1470 Ferrara Miscellany.[11]

8. In this 1470 Ferrara Miscellany, another Jewish prayer book, we find Judith presented close to Judas Maccabeus. This reflects the connection between Judith and Hanukkah. Here too we may observe the delimitation of the presentation of the story. Only one scene is presented, and it is that of Judith waving her sword and beheading Holofernes.

9. The same may be seen in an Armenian manuscript of the seventh century from Constantinople (figure 4).[12] As in the Jewish manuscript, Judith is standing in the tent with her servant, a sword in one hand and the severed head in the other. As in most of the Armenian manuscripts, here too the story of Judith appears as a marginal illumination. Here the absence of Holofernes is notable. The only figures are Judith, the servant and the head. Below we shall see how this branch of the presentation of the story developed.

B. The Epitomized Description -- the Moment of Decapitation.

The moment that caught the imagination of many of the greatest plastic artists was the moment of Holofernes' decapitation by Judith as a symbol of all the detailed Judith story. This approach starts already in the eleventh-twelfth centuries, when we find an expansion of the description of the Judith story on the one hand, and, on the other, a concentration and epitomizing of the story to the single scene of the decapitation, presenting only Judith with the sword, and Holofernes at her feet. Examples are particularly common in Western art, in sculpture, in stained glass, in manuscripts, and even in tapestries.

1. In the eleventh-century Italian manuscript Codex Barberini we find the first known example that looks as if it was cut out of a larger, more complex scene (figure 5).[13] It is a copy of a narrative model, like those preceding, but there is a concentration on the moment of the decapitation, with Judith represented laying her sword on Holofernes' neck. This had been a common subject, it seems, in Byzantine models, and from there it passed to Western art.

2. In the West this symbolic representation was accepted enthusiastically and the scene appears regularly in margins, as in the Armenian example given above, or in the illuminated initial letter of the book of Judith. This latter type of representation was particularly common. Sometimes the letter even represented a tent (figure 6).[14]

3. Although there are many representations of the moment of the decapitation itself, there are even more frequent examples of the following moment, when the head is already severed from the body. This could be illustrated in numerous examples down to Donatello's famous sculpture.[15]

4. Other rarer scenes are Judith's immersion and her prayer before setting out. A fine example of her prayer appears in the Cathedral of Chartres in the thirteenth century, in the right portal of the north transept. Here she is kneeling down in prayer (figure 7).[16]

5. There are also other Judith scenes such as her putting on sackcloth, placing dust on her head, and changing her clothes. A good example of these occurs in a Latin Psalter from Munich of the twelfth-thirteenth century.[17]

The story covers two pages, each of which has three registers divided into smaller scenes. At the top left is a complex scene showing Judith's preparations to leave Bethulia: her prayer, the servant kneeling beside Judith who is dressed in sackcloth and putting ashes on her head. On the lower left the servant is watching Judith who is praying and immersing herself before going to Holofernes.

On the second page, on the right lower one sees Judith's burial, a very rare scene (the other scenes are their departure, their coming to Holofernes, the murder, and the feast).

C. The Expanded Description in the Twelfth Century.

Concurrent with the concentration of the figure of Judith to one symbolic scene, there also developed a type of representation which expanded the story. This is not a question of registers on one or two pages, but a detailed representation over a number of pages, sometimes as many as seven or more.

1. A good example is the Velislaus Bible, a Czech Picture Book of the Bible which dates from the fourteenth century and has an extensive Judith cycle.[18]

2. An earlier example of the expanded representation is the Pampalona Bible of 1200.[19] In the Pampalona Bible, the story of Judith takes a number of pages. The most interesting of all the scenes is that in which Judith brings the head to the elders of Bethulia. Here Judith appears in a new way, as victor and vanquisher of Satan in the form of Holofernes. The scene describes Judith's presentation of Holofernes' head to the elders of the city, all of whom stand above the image of Satan who is falling and declining, and next to him is written the word "Lucifer."

Clear examples of this idea may be found, for instance, in the writings of Rabanus Maurus, in his Expositio in Librum Judith or in the sermons of Bonaventura who calls Nebuchadnezzar Satan, Holofernes his emissary, and Antiochus Epiphanes the serpent.[20] In the medieval Christian liturgy, Judith is always mentioned together with other figures who symbolized the weak overcoming the mighty: David, the Maccabees, Jael, Mordecai, and Esther. It is natural that also in art she should stand by these figures.

3. Alternatively she was herself presented as the figure of the Victor trampling Satan underfoot, as did Christ or the Virgin. In the twelfth-century Speculum Virginum, Judith and Jael trample their enemies while Humilitas tramples Superbia. (Note the branches Judith holds, according to Jdt 15:12 [figure 8].)[21]

The interesting presentation of Judith trampling Satan who appears as Holofernes' head reminds us of other scenes in art which represent this phenomenon, namely, the Harrowing of Hell, in which Christ tramples Satan in Hades as he ascends from Limbo (figure 9).[22] This phenomenon also appears in the scene of the Baptism in which the painter, either consciously or in unconscious copying, represents Christ's victory over Satan who is trying to steal the baptismal water. Sometimes Satan himself appears, and more frequently there is a misapprehension of the personification of the river.[23]

It is said that until man is baptized, Satan tries to put the baptism off and to steal the baptismal water, since baptism is a victory over Satan. Ideas of this type may be found in different liturgies and in early Christian writing. In all these liturgies the attempt is to purify the water from Satan and put him to flight.[24] In places in which the painter was conscious of the meaning of the scene, he in some instances set crosses into the water to help in the victory over Satan.[25]

D. The Symbolic Figure - the Sword and the Head.

In the period in which Judith was a prefiguration of the Victory over Satan and according to that concept, it was natural that the figure of Judith moved from its original religious context and became meaningful in a similar, but secular, context. Indeed, the motive of courage shifted the essence of the story of Judith to a new image. The act of decapitation itself became the subject of a new scene: Judith, the sword and the head (or at least one of the two) in her hand.

1. The beginnings of this iconography may be detected in the eleventh century in an Italian Bible where, as a summary of the book, Judith appears with her sword wielded in her right hand and the head in her left.[26] Here we should recall the meaning of the different hands in the iconography of Christ who always blesses with his right hand. In the scene of the Last Judgment he blesses those entering Paradise with his right hand and those going to Hell with his left.

2. Although it is possible to present numerous examples from the eleventh and succeeding centuries, we shall pass directly to the fifteenth century, to the Gates of the Garden of Eden, which are the bronze gates made by Ghiberti in Florence in 1450.[27]

Here Judith stands in a similar position, a sword in her right hand, the symbol of her courage, and the head in her left, the symbol of the evil which has been overcome. Henceforth this becomes a standard image in art for courage and patriotic rebellion. On the doors here shown Judith is next to a panel which describes David's war against the Philistines. This conjunction with David, both weak people against strong, saviors of their nation, inspired Donatello to make his statue (figure 10).[28]

3. In the Renaissance Judith appears in the work of the greatest artists -- Botticelli, Mantegnia, Giorgionne, Tintoretto and others. We are particularly interested, however, in those who showed the way towards the patriotic presentation of Judith. Donatello added Civic Virtue to all

Judith's usual characteristics. Both this statue and the one that he had done 30 years earlier of David with Goliath's head at his feet were commissioned by the Medici family in Florence. When they were expelled, the two statues were moved to the main square of the city, where they became symbols of the Florentines' struggle for independence and freedom. These virtues, then, were also seen in Judith as victor. On the podium of the statue was engraved "Kingdoms fall through Luxury; Cities rise through Virtue: Behold the Neck of Pride severed by the hand of Humility."

This inscription no longer survives, but it is described in contemporary documents. Here the theological tradition of the victory of Humility over Pride is expressed as well as ideals of civic freedom and courage.[29]

The image of Judith, dressed, trampling the naked body of her enemy takes us back to the image of Christ trampling Satan and of Mary acting in the same way. These images now appear in a new form : Virtues trampling Vices. Holofernes, who is naked and cast down on the pillow, represents Lust while Judith is Humility just as in the illumination from the twelfth century, when Judith and Jael trample their enemies, who look like the Satan of the Resurrection Scene. Between them there is a personification of Humility trampling Lust (the branches that she took in her hand according to 15:12 are interesting in this connection).[30]

4. Here, in the fifteenth century, we shall pause a little and ask ourselves what happens in Jewish art. So far, we have examined Christian art, but Judith is not just a Jewish woman but also the symbol of the Jewish people--of their victory over their enemies, of their deliverance by a woman but with the help of Israel's God.

In the fifteenth century, together with the patriotic-national development of the Judith figure in Catholic Italy, this figure appears in Jewish art as well. Here too, it is placed in the context of the patriotic dimension of the national revolt for independence, i.e. in connection with the Story of the Maccabees. This book served as the source and basis of a number of midrashim and Piyyutim in the Middle Ages and particularly those for Hanukkah.[31]

5. A number of Passover Haggadot show Judith also in association with the Passover story, like the Prague Haggada of 1526 (figure 11).[32] This shows the passage, "Pour out your wrath upon the nations," positioning

Judith alongside Samson on the right, who is carrying the lintels he has uprooted.

6. European Jews in the fifteenth-sixteenth centuries, particularly in Italy, were also open to the nationalist ideas which influenced Gentile society and which were concentrated in the figure of Judith. This figure was taken over by the Jews of that age and that area, the more so for Judith's association with the period of the Maccabean revolt. The view that she was of the Hasmonean family turned her into a popular figure on Italian Hanukkah candelabra. The figure of Judith sometimes replaces meaningful symbols like the crown of the Torah over the Ark of the Torah.[33]

The Great Transformation

From this point on a great change takes place; the figure of Judith gradually changes direction and a new image alters the fighting figure of the fifteenth-sixteenth centuries. A biblical topic received a secular content: the faithfulness to her people, which had brought about her sacrifice and courage and which had been prominent to this time, became a new sort of faithfulness. Motifs of the triumph of Love affect the woodcuts and the tapestries that were made for the houses of the wealthy.

In these works there were presented series of couples, the woman of which carries out a betrayal for the sake of her beloved. Fixed members of these series are scenes with Adam and Eve, with Samson and Delilah, with David and Bathsheba, with Jezebel and Ahab, and with Salome and John the Baptist. To this series of pairs are added outstanding women who endangered their lives for their people, such as Jael with Sisera, Esther with Ahasuerus, Susanna with the Elders, and Judith with Holofernes.

These were not sinful women, but women who because of their betrayal of men who trusted them were worthy of being abandoned. Judith was one of this list in spite of explicitly being called righteous and in spite of having yielded herself to no man. Her only offense was to be a woman who dared to kill a man. The chief argument of those who wished to remove Donatello's Judith from the public square in Florence was that it was not appropriate for a woman to kill a man.[34]

1. A good example of the change in the image of Judith is the realistic cool and brutal look on Caravaggio's Judith in his painting of the early seventeenth century. The blood is gushing out of Holofernes' neck while Judith and her maid, looking like a witch, are watching (figure 12).[35]

2. A personal touch in this direction was supplied by Christofano Allori who in 1609 painted Judith with the head in her hand and the servant by her side.[36] However, this picture also reflects the personal story of the painter who fell in love with a local beauty and spent all his money on her. His jealousy and their fights were public knowledge. In the picture, Judith is this woman, whose face is cold and unyielding in spite of the horrible thing she is holding. The head is a self-portrait of Allori himself, whose features express deep pain. The servant is the Italian beauty's mother (figure 13).[37]

3. In modern art this process continues, but all this development is limited to Christian art. In Jewish art, Judith never ceased being the figure of faithfulness to her people and of heroism and sacrifice for them. She continued as a heroine of the Feast of Hanukkah beyond the candelabra. Even one of the most modern Jewish artists is faithful to the traditional figure of Judith. The American Jewish painter, Leonard Baskin in "Chosen Days" represented in 1981 various festivals by biblical figures. Esther is Purim, Ruth is Shavuot, and Judith is Hanukkah. The reason is doubtless the continued use of medieval Jewish texts and Piyyutim for Hanukkah which preserved the figure of Judith in the Jewish tradition (figure 14).[38]

[1]This paper forms part of a more extensive ongoing study of mine on the figure of Judith in art.

[2]See F. Saxl, "Warburg's Visit to New Mexico," Lectures, (unpublished) 1.328; 2, pl. 233b.

[3]See B. Bayer, Encyclopaedia Judaica, s.v. "Judith."

[4]F.G. Godwin, "The Judith Illustrations of the 'Hortus Deliciarum,'" Gazette des Beaux Arts 36 (1949) figure 4. This article has been particularly helpful in the present research, and it provides much of the basic information we have used in this paper.

[5]Manuscript Vat. Gr. 1, fol. 383, shown in Godwin, "Judith Illustrations," fig. 2.

[6]Bibliothèque nationale, Paris ms. lat. fol. 134v; see Godwin, "Judith Illustrations," figures 5, 6, and 15.

[7]On the Arsenal Bible, see H. Buchthal, Miniature Painting in the Latin Kingdom of Jerusalem (Oxford: Oxford University Press, 1957) 54-68 and pl. 73.

[8]See R.S. Kramer, ed., Maenads, Martyrs, Matrons, Monastics (Philadelphia: Fortress, 1988) 235.

[9]See Godwin, "Judith Illustrations," 25-28 and figure 1.

[10]The Hamburg Miscellany, in Hamburg, Staats- und Universitätsbibliothek, Cod. Heb. 37 (Mainz?), 1434 CE fol. 81.

[11]The Rothschild Miscellany, Jerusalem, Israel Museum, 180/51, fol. 217. Ferrara, 1470-1480.

[12]Jerusalem, Armenian Patriarchate, Ms. 1927, fol. 219b.

[13]Barberini Codex, Rome, vat. lat 587: see Godwin, "Judith Illustrations," figure 3.

[14]Bible of Stephen Harding III, fol. 158; Dijon bibl. commun., mss. 12-15: see Godwin, "Judith Illustrations," figure 17.

[15]Examples are the following: (a) Rome, vat. lat. 12958: see Godwin, "Judith Illustrations," figure 9; (b) Encyclopaedia Judaica 10.454, figure 2; (c) Encyclopaedia Judaica 10.454, figure 1; (d) R.M. Whittkover, Born Under Saturn (London: Weidenfeld and Nicholson, 1963) pl. 48; (e) Donatello's sculpture which is discussed below.

[16]R. Branner, Chartres Cathedral (New York: Norton, 1969), figure 89.

[17]See HBC 808.

[18]We are preparing a much more extended study of this cycle. On the manuscript, see A. Matějček, Velislavova Bible (Prague: Jan Stenc, 1926).

[19]F. Bucher, The Pampalona Bibles (New Haven and London: Yale University Press, 1970) vol. 1, figure 123.

[20]M. Friedman, "The Metamorphoses of Judith," Jewish Art 12-13 (1986-87) 233, nn. 31-32.

[21]London, British Library, Arundel 44, fol 34v (twelfth century): see also E. Greenhill, Speculum Virginum (New York: 1962) 234-235, pl. 12 (non vidi).

[22]V. Lazarev, Storia della Pittura bizantina (Torino: Guilio Einaudi, 1967), figure 337. On the early version in Ravenna, see also A.D. Kartsonis, Anastasis (Princeton: Princeton University Press, 1986).

[23]J.B. Russell, Satan (Ithaca and London: Cornell University Press, 1988), pl. 191. See also S. Der Nersessian, Armenian Manuscripts in the Walters Art Gallery (Baltimore: Walters Art Gallery, 1973) figure 200. My study on this feature will be published shortly.

[24]Ideas of this type may be found in the writings of Origen. See Russell, Satan, 142-43, n.99; the Latin Catholic liturgy: see J.B. Russell, Lucifer (Ithaca and London: Cornell University Press, 1986) 127, n.74; the Armenian liturgy; see Der Nersessian, Walters Art Gallery, 38, 49.

[25]Der Nersessian, Walters Art Gallery, figure 143.

[26]See Godwin, "Judith Illustrations," figure 7.

[27]Friedman, "Metamorphoses," figure 15.

[28]Encyclopaedia Judaica 10.454, figure 1.

[29]H.W. Jansen, The Sculpture of Donatello (Princeton: Princeton University Press, 1957) 198.

[30]Godwin, "Judith Illustrations," figure 12. See also Kartsonis, Anastasis.

[31]Encyclopaedica Judaica 10.460.

[32]R.Ch. Wengrov, Haddadah and Woodcut (New York: Shulsinger Brothers, 1967) 65-71.

[33]Encyclopaedica Judaica 10.456, figure 6.

[34]Janson, Donatello, 30.

[35]Rome, Palazzo Barberini by Caravaggio (1571-1610).

[36]Whittkover, Born Under Saturn, 160-61, pl. 48.

[37]Unusual representations of Judith's story appeared from time to time, like the one from the eleventh century in which Judith looks like the victim and Holofernes' head like the victor. Note the changed role of Judith's hands in this painting. See H. Swarzenski, Vorgotische Miniaturen (Leipzig: Karl Robert Langewiesche, 1931) 45.

[38]See Catalogue of the Schilman Collection of Twentieth-Century American Art (New York: Jewish Museum, 1985) 16, number 5.

Figure 2: The Arsenal Bible
5211 folio 252r
(thirteenth century)

Figure 1: Bible of St. Paul
folio 231r (ninth century)

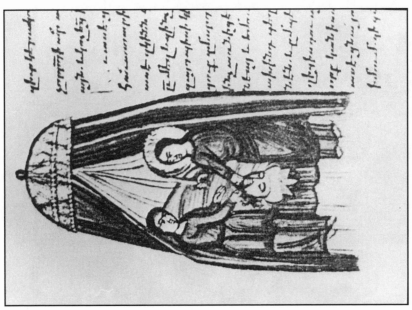

Figure 4: Armenian Ms.
(seventeenth century)

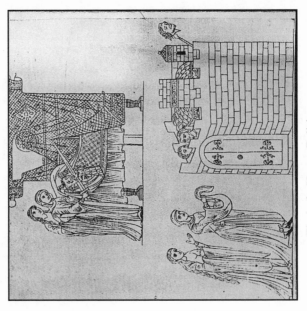

Figure 3: Hortus Deliciarum
folio 60 (twelfth century)

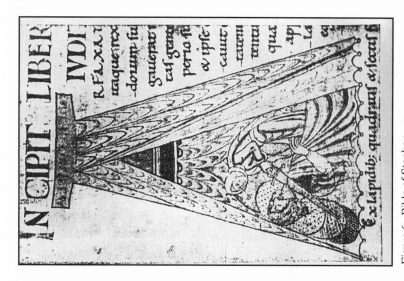

Figure 6: Bible of Stephen Harding (twelfth century)

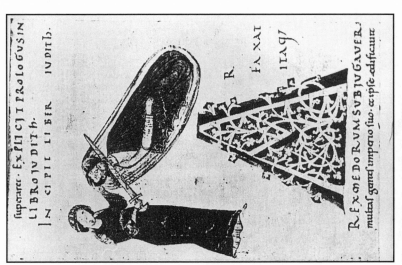

Figure 5: Barberini Codex 1097

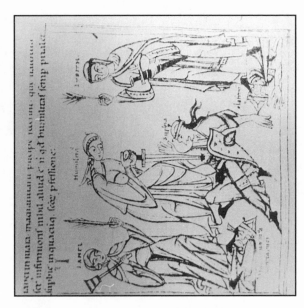

Figure 8: Speculum Virginum
(twelfth century)

Figure 7: From Chartres Cathedral
(thirteenth century)

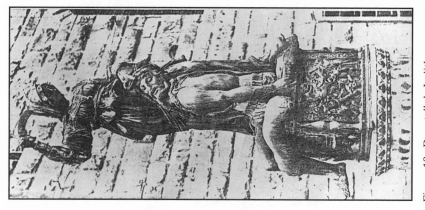

Figure 10: Donatello's Judith
and Holofernes, Bronze (1455-57)

Figure 9: Anastasis
(twelfth century)

Figure 12: Carravagio's Judith
and Holofernes (1571-1610)

Figure 11: The Prague Haggada
(1526)

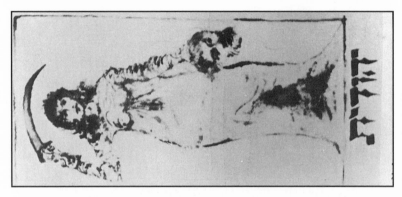

Figure 14: L. Baskin,
Chosen Days (1981)

Figure 13: Allori's Judith
and Holofernes (1609)